THE SECRET TEACHINGS OF CHRIST

based on the parables

SHAHAN SHAMMAS

WORTHWHILE PUBLICATIONS

Copyright © 2025 SHAHAN SHAMMAS

Copyright © 2025 by Shahan Shammas. All rights reserved. No part of this book may be reproduced or transmitted in any form or by any means, electronic or mechanical, including photocopying, recording, or by an information storage and retrieval system–except by a reviewer who may quote brief passages in a review to be printed in a book, magazine or newspaper–without permission in writing from the publisher. For information, please contact Worthwhile Publications or the author at shahanshammas@gmail.com

Although the author and publisher have made every effort to ensure the accuracy and completeness of information contained in this book, we assume no responsibility for errors, inaccuracies, omissions, or any inconsistencies herein. Any slights on people, places, or organizations are unintentional.

ISBN-13: 9780966202847

To my wife, Barbara, and my daughters Olivia and Emily and their husbands Ben and Antony. To my grandchildren Dylan and Chloe. To the brave souls everywhere who are unafraid to question their beliefs, open their eyes to see, clear their ears to hear and examine their hearts to discern the truth.

CONTENTS

Title Page
Copyright
Dedication
Introduction   1
Why Parables?   6
Parable of the Lamp   15
Parable of the Speck and the Log   21
Parable of the New Cloth on an Old Garment   27
Parable of the Divided Kingdom   38
Parable of the Sower   46
Parable of the Weeds   56
Mystery of the Kingdom of Heaven   63
Parable of the Heart of Man   83
Parable of The Lost Sheep   93
Parable of The Unforgiving Servant   100
Parable of the Laborers in the Vineyard   105
Parable of the Prodigal Son   112
Parable of the Tenants   119
Parable of the Wedding Feast   128
Parable of the Barren Fig Tree   135
Parable of the Faithful vs. the Wicked Servant   142

Parable of the Ten Virgins	147
Parable of the Talents	158
Parable of the Good Samaritan	168
Parable of the Friend at Midnight	176
Parable of the Rich Fool	182
Parable of the Invited Guest	188
Parable of the Lost Coin	193
Parable of the Rich Man and Lazarus	198
Parable of the Persistent Widow	204
Parable of the Pharisee and the Tax Collector	209
The Life of Jesus Christ as a Parable	215
The Last Supper as a Parable	227
Summary	240
Conclusion	248
Appendix A	251
Appendix B	264
Appendix C	269
Acknowledgement	281
About The Author	283

INTRODUCTION

We do not know what Christ taught His disciples in secret because it was never written down. What we have are the parables.

The parables reveal what has been hidden from us—The Secret Teachings of Christ. To see this message clearly, and to hear His words distinctly, we need an open mind and a pure desire to know and understand.

The parables appear to be simple stories that Christ told His listeners. They are encoded with hidden gems of truth that Christ could not reveal openly lest He be stoned and killed prematurely. The parables are a clever way to preserve His teachings for posterity. The time has come to openly reveal these truths and secrets for all.

This book will reveal the secret teachings of Christ based on the parables.

To grasp the full significance of what is hidden in the parables, our intention must be clear and we must be fearless. We are told that fear of God is the beginning of wisdom. It is not. Fear never leads to wisdom; pure love and fearless action do.

* * * * *

I take continuous education seriously. I have spent most of my adult life learning. I have read countless non-fiction books, attended many self-improvement programs and given numerous lectures, seminars and workshops myself. Lately, I have been streaming courses from the **"The Great Courses"** website. I have purchased over 60 of their programs. One of these Great Courses is **"The Greatest Controversies of Early Christian History"** by Bart Ehrman, PhD, Professor at The University of North Carolina, Chapel Hill. Dr. Ehrman discusses many controversies of the early Christian Church. Was Jesus human and then became divine? Was He divine and then incarnated as a human? Was He both human and God? Was Mary a virgin? Is Paul the real founder of Christianity? Did the disciples write the Bible? Does the New Testament contain forgeries? And many other controversies.

We do not have many historical facts regarding Jesus. Even the statements attributed to Him might not be reliable, but what we can rely on are His parables. These are simple stories meant to convey a moral or to reveal a spiritual truth. Stories are easy to remember and are a simple way to preserve their core meaning. Our interest in the parables is not the outer meaning, but rather what these parables contain that ordinary eyes cannot see.

Parables transcend time and their insightful messages are as applicable today as they were in the days of Christ. They are embedded with gems of truth and are loaded with valuable lessons that we can use in our daily lives.

We know that Christ taught the public via parables. We also know that He taught His disciples openly and with detailed explanations. What we do not know is what these private or secret teachings were. They were specifically for the disciples and those prepared by Christ to receive His teachings. Unless we become one of His disciples ourselves, we cannot access these secret teachings. Fortunately, we can do this by allowing inspiration from the Holy Spirit to engulf and infuse us as it did for the disciples during the Pentecost.

This book will reveal many of those secret teachings. These are the gems of truth and the valuable lessons embedded within the parables.

Some of the topics this book will cover are:

- What lessons can we learn from the parable of the lamp?
- What does John the Baptist symbolize?
- Why can't we mix new and old garments?
- What is meant by the "Old" and the" New"?
- Who are Beelzebub and Satan?
- Where is the most fertile soil to sow spiritual seeds and who is the Sower?
- What exactly is the Kingdom of Heaven? Is it within us? How do we find and use it? Why is the Kingdom of Heaven like a seed, yeast, a treasure, a pearl and a net? How can discovering the Kingdom Within transform our lives?
- Why did Christ have 12 disciples?
- Why would a shepherd leave 99 of his sheep to seek the one he lost?
- Why must we forgive?
- How can we double the talents we are entrusted with?
- Who is the Prodigal Son who returns home?
- Did Christ come to die for our sins? Or did we kill Him because of our sins?
- Why would Christ expect a barren fig tree to produce figs? What "fertilizer" can we use to be productive ourselves?
- Why does Christ refer to "wedding feasts" in His parables? Who is invited to these feasts?
- Why 10 virgins?
- What is the significance of the numbers Christ used in His parables?
- Why is the parable of The Good Samaritan so important?
- Who is our neighbor?
- What does "midnight" refer to in the parables?

- Is it possible to be rich and be saved?
- Are Heaven and Hell real places?
- What secrets lie hidden in The Lord's Last Supper?
- What does the life of Jesus Christ tell us about our lives?

It has been 2 millennia since Jesus Christ appeared in Palestine and revealed His message of love, hope and compassion. The world was in desperate need of His message then, as we are for the same message now. When Jesus first revealed His teachings, most rejected His message outright. Even those who knew Him, in His hometown, rejected Him.

Jesus Rejected at Nazareth, His Hometown

And when Jesus had finished these parables, he went away from there, and coming to his hometown he taught them in their synagogue, so that they were astonished, and said, "Where did this man get this wisdom and these mighty works? Is not this the carpenter's son? Is not his mother called Mary? And are not his brothers James and Joseph and Simon and Judas? And are not all his sisters with us? Where then did this man get all these things?" And they took offense at him. But Jesus said to them, "A prophet is not without honor except in his hometown and in his own household." And he did not do many mighty works there, because of their unbelief. Matt 13:53-58

We have come a long way since the days of Christ. Hopefully, we have advanced, not only technically, but spiritually as well and we are ready to accept what Christ could not teach openly then. We rejected Him then. Let us not do it again.

The hidden messages of Christ as revealed in His parables are powerful, insightful and transformative. They have the power to alter not only our lives, but the entire world as well. Like the seed that needs to be planted, and like the yeast that must be embedded in dough, the teachings of Christ must fall as seeds into the soil of our hearts and minds. We must prepare our soil to be fertile by having eyes that see, ears that hear and hearts that feel.

It is time to put the Old "truths" behind us and embrace the New "truths."

The secrets hidden in the parables are about to be revealed.

Are we ready to receive them?

WHY PARABLES?

Every happening, great and small, is a parable whereby God speaks to us, and the art of life is to get the message.
—Malcolm Muggeridge

Telling stories has been a way of life for a long time. When I was a child, I listened to my dad telling stories. I never knew whether he made them up or if he remembered them from his predecessors. I did not see any deep or hidden meaning in any of those stories. I enjoyed them for what they were, stories to entertain and to pass time. As long as I remained a child, I could not see anything else in the stories. It is only after I grew up and had a larger perspective that I began to see the hidden and deeper meaning hidden in some of those stories. There are three types of stories:

1. Regular Stories
2. Myths and
3. Parables.

Regular stories are meant to amuse, entertain and to socialize.

Myths are traditional stories about heroes or supernatural beings, often attempting to explain the origins of natural phenomena or aspects of human behavior.

Parables are short simple stories intended to illustrate a moral or to impart a religious lesson.

The myths and parables that the spiritual teachers left us are gifts bequeathed to posterity. These gifts are wrapped and their inner contents are hidden from us. They must be unwrapped and evaluated to reveal their deeper and hidden meaning. And that is what I intend to do with the parables of Christ.

Continuing the ancient tradition, Christ taught in parables. What Christ meant by a parable is different than what the average person understood by that parable. His audience was incapable of understanding His lofty messages. This is why He said to His disciples that He can only teach the people in parables, but to them, He can teach the truth openly.

Christ was an exceptional parable teller. He not only hid His most important teachings in these parables, but he also had another purpose for telling them. He wanted us to:

    a. Live the abundant life as if we are at a wedding feast;
    b. Transform our everyday challenges into opportunities;
    c. Move from the Old culture that fosters acrimonious relationships due to belief, race, gender and differences to a New culture that nurtures harmonious coexistence;
    d. Eliminate intolerance and violence from our lives;
    e. Remove the concept of "enemies" from our minds.

Christ could not teach publicly because metaphysical ideas are not for everyone. The vast majority of people are not interested in these ideas. They are in survival mode. Only a few are metaphysically inclined. To preserve and transmit these, it is best to use stories, allegories, parables, rituals, symbols, and cryptic writings. When Christ wanted to explain something to the people, he told them parables. When He wanted to speak openly, He confided in His disciples. All the parables come from

Matthew, Mark and Luke. There are no parables in the Gospel according to John. I have also included parables from The Gospel of Thomas.

We can interpret the parables of Christ in 4 ways.

The first is the simple interpretation. We basically accept the parables as they are. The Gnostics called this level of interpretation **Hylic** or the simple and material level. At this level, we accept the parables at face value and view them as literal truth and as historic fact. Many do just that. That is their prerogative and it is not wrong, but that's just one way of interpreting sacred writings—surface understanding, blind to the deeper, hidden meaning.

The second way to view the parables is to see the deeper meaning in them and realize that they are symbolic, figurative, and allegorical. The Gnostics called this level of interpretation **Psychic** or the mental level. At this level, we realize that these parables are allegories. In other words, they stand for something else and there is a deeper hidden truth. This truth is not self-evident; it must be unwrapped.

The third way to view parables is the spiritual level. The Gnostics called this level **Pneumatic**. At this level we realize there is a hidden, deeper, and spiritual meaning to the parables. We understand that these parables contain profound spiritual laws and truths. The spiritual meaning of a parable is often hidden; hence it is called esoteric. The literal and mundane meaning is evident and obvious; hence, it is called exoteric.

The fourth and final way to view parables is the personal level. Here we cease to interpret and analyze. We simply know that the parables are about us. We understand them based on our own personal experiences. As we unravel the hidden meanings in these parables, we have a Gnosis. We simply know what the parables mean and why Christ told them.

Why did Christ teach the public in parables?

All these things Jesus said to the crowds in parables; indeed, he said nothing to them without a parable. This was to fulfill what was spoken by the prophet: "I will open my mouth in parables; I will utter what has been hidden since the foundation of the world." Matt 13:34-35

Obviously, it is not true that Jesus said nothing to the crowds except through parables.

What about the Sermon on the Mount and all of His other sayings? These are not parables.

Christ spoke to the general public in parables and general statements. This book is not about His general statements. It is about the parables and the hidden gems buried deep within them.

"I will utter what has been hidden since the foundation of the world." Matt 13:35

Christ used parables for three main reasons:

1. Fear of persecution

If Christ had taught people openly stating what He really wanted to say, He would run the risk of being persecuted. Even with the little that He did expose, He was tried, tortured and crucified. People did not like to have their beliefs challenged. They did not like to be exposed as frauds and hypocrites. Persecution runs deep in the psyche of humanity. Many religions, including Christianity, engaged in horrendous persecutions of anyone they accused of heresy.

We believe that we live in an enlightened age. Far from it. Admittedly, there are pockets of enlightenment the world over. However, there are vast areas of darkness where ignorance, superstition and fear rule the day. People have not changed much since the days of Christ. Christ refers to them in Matthew 13:13-15.

> *This is why I speak to them in parables, because seeing they do not see, and hearing they do not hear, nor do they understand. Indeed, in their case the prophecy of Isaiah is fulfilled that says:*
>
> *"You will indeed hear but never understand, and you will indeed see but never perceive." For this people's heart has grown dull, and with their ears they can barely hear, and their eyes they have closed, lest they should see with their eyes and hear with their ears and understand with their heart and turn, and I would heal them.'*

2. To conceal gems of truth for future generations

If the people of His generation were unable to understand and appreciate the teachings of Christ, then perhaps future generations can and will. Parables are an excellent way to convey spiritual truths in the guise of simple stories. The gems hidden in these parables must be extracted, polished and exposed to the light of reason, analysis and contemplation. Concealing esoteric truths in parables avoids persecution and preserves the knowledge for future generations.

3. To enhance accuracy

Nothing Christ did or said was written down as it happened. The stories about Christ were transmitted orally from person to person and from one generation to the next. The first gospel, Mark, was not written down until about 40 years after the death of Christ. Nobody knows who actually wrote the gospels. They are attributed to Matthew, Mark, Luke and John. Matthew and John are the only disciples who personally knew Christ and are eye witnesses. Unfortunately, (according to Bart Ehrman, PH. D) they did not write the two gospels attributed to them. The disciples of Christ were simple fishermen. They spoke Aramaic and were almost illiterate. They had no knowledge of Greek, the language in which the gospels were written. They could not have composed such literary works as the gospels.

We cannot trust the accuracy of the statements in the gospels. There have been numerous translations, additions, deletions and even forgeries. Here is an example of an addition about a statement in the gospels regarding Peter and what Christ said about him. This quotation is from Barbara Walker author of **_The Women's Encyclopedia of Myths and Secrets_**.

> *"The myth of St. Peter was the slender thread from which hung the whole weighty structure of the Roman papacy. One solitary passage in the Gospel of Matthew said Jesus made a pun by giving Simon son of Jonah the new name of Peter, "Rock" (Latin petra), saying he would found his church on this rock (Matthew 16:18-19).*
>
> *Unfortunately for papal credibility, the so-called Petrine passage was a forgery. It was deliberately inserted into the scripture about the 3rd century A.D. as a political ploy, to uphold the primacy of the Roman see against rival churches in the east. Various Christian bishoprics were engaged in a power struggle in which the chief weapons were bribery, forgery, and intrigue, with elaborate fictions and hoaxes written into sacred books, and ruthless competition between rival parties for the lucrative position of God's elite."*

What we can trust in the gospels are the parables. These are simple stories that preserve their core accuracy as they are told and retold from one generation to the next. While the stories might vary slightly, the intangible truth hidden in the parables remains preserved.

It was not only Christ who could not speak and teach openly. This was the fate of all advanced thinkers, innovators and trendsetters. People either did not have the intellectual capacity to understand, or if they did, they would persecute the teacher. Below are two quotes by Paul:

> *But I, brothers, could not address you as spiritual people, but as people of the flesh, as infants in Christ. I fed you with milk, not solid food, for you were not ready for it. And even now you are not yet ready, for you are still of the flesh. For while there is jealousy and strife among you, are you not of the flesh and behaving only in a human way? For when one says, "I follow Paul," and another, "I follow Apollos," are you not being merely human? 1 Corinthians 3:1-4*

> *About this we have much to say, and it is hard to explain, since you have become dull of hearing. For though by this time you ought to be teachers, you need someone to teach you again the basic principles of the oracles of God. You need milk, not solid food, for everyone who lives on milk is unskilled in the word of righteousness, since he is a child. But solid food is for the mature, for those who have their powers of discernment trained by constant practice to distinguish good from evil. Hebrew 5:11-14*

Biblical experts know which of the stories in the Bible have a historical basis and which ones are mere fables without any foundation in reality. Christ stated that everything He taught publicly were parables. There is a statement in Galatians that even the stories in the Old Testament might have been mere parables intended to convey a moral or teach a lesson.

Hagar and Sarah as a parable

> *Tell me, you who desire to be under the law, do you not listen to the law? For it is written that Abraham had two sons, one by a slave woman and one by a free woman. But the son of the slave was born according to the flesh, while the son of the free woman was born through promise. Now*

> *this may be interpreted allegorically: these women are two covenants. One is from Mount Sinai, bearing children for slavery; she is Hagar. Now Hagar is Mount Sinai in Arabia; she corresponds to the present Jerusalem, for she is in slavery with her children. But the Jerusalem above is free, and she is our mother. For it is written, "Rejoice, O barren one who does not bear; break forth and cry aloud, you who are not in labor! For the children of the desolate one will be more than those of the one who has a husband." Gal 4: 21-27*

Christ could not teach the people what He wanted them to know. They had eyes but could not see. They had ears but could not hear. Their hearts were hard like stone so they could not feel. A veil of ignorance, superstition and fear was preventing them from being spiritually alive. Like children needing milk, not solid food, Paul and Christ could only use allegories and parables to teach. They were hoping the day will come when the veil will lift and the people will be resurrected to spiritual life. When that happens, we become the blessed who see, hear and understand.

> *But blessed are your eyes, for they see, and your ears, for they hear. For truly, I say to you, many prophets and righteous people longed to see what you see, and did not see it, and to hear what you hear, and did not hear it. Matt 13:10-17*

Three Important Gifts from Christ Through the Parables

1. Love and acceptance

Several parables make it clear that we are loved beyond measure. We are accepted regardless of what we may have done or did not do. We will be welcomed home with open arms once we decide to head back home.

2. Sense of responsibility

Several parables make it clear that we are responsible for our lives. We have been gifted with talents, skills and abilities. These must be put to good use for a multiple return. Our responsibility extends to our thoughts, feelings, actions and lives.

3. Self-esteem

Being loved should boost our self-esteem, so should being accepted for who we are. Accepting and loving ourselves will enhance our self-confidence. Instead of embracing demeaning beliefs such as original sin, we should celebrate the fact that we are loved and esteemed. Our "shepherd" would gladly leave His 99 sheep behind and search for us, the lost ones, until we are found. Then, he will rejoice and we will celebrate together.

PARABLE OF THE LAMP

If you light a lamp for somebody, it will also brighten your path. —Gautama Buddha

The Parable

You are the light of the world. A city set on a hill cannot be hidden. Nor do people light a lamp and put it under a basket, but on a stand, and it gives light to all in the house. In the same way, let your light shine before others, so that they may see your good works and give glory to your Father who is in heaven. Matt 5:14-16

The Hidden Meaning

This is an incredibly loaded and powerful parable. First of all, it is an ego booster. Imagine Christ telling us what we are—the light of the world. But what good is a light if it remains hidden? We hide our light under the guises of fear, uncertainty, timidity and most importantly, ignorance of our power to make a difference.

Christ wants us to shine our light brightly, from the mountain top, unhindered by any obstacles. He wants us to share our light with others. We can do this best by being a lighthouse and radiating our brightness wherever we happen to be. Thus, we automatically dispel darkness by our mere presence. Others will feel the warmth of our light and they will be impacted.

Being a light requires us to be fearless, for we need to expose all forms of darkness—hate, unfairness, mistreatment, prejudice, and ignorance. Christ wants us to reveal what the unscrupulous do to hide their malevolent acts under good pretenses. He wants us to expose the dark secrets of the powerful who impose their will on the weak. By shining our light brightly, we speed up our spiritual growth.

Christ equates the lamp within with the eyes.

> *"The eye is the lamp of the body. So, if your eye is healthy, your whole body will be full of light. Matt 6:22 (ESV2011)*

The King James's version of this verse equates the lamp with light.

> *The light of the body is the eye: if therefore thine eye be single, thy whole body shall be full of light. Matt 6:22 (KJV)*

The eyes were very important for the ancients. They are very important even today. Eye contact between infant and mother establishes an enduring bond between them. The eyes enable us to see, not only physically, but also as a source of intuitive vision.

Christ tells us that our eyes are the lamps of our bodies. Our eyes are "healthy" when we know what to look at, what to focus on and what to ignore. In other words, we must train our eyes to see beauty where there is ugliness and opportunity where there is an obstacle. Our eyes are "bad" when all we see and focus on is negativity, lack and imperfections. Instead of criticizing, why not see the good and the positive?

Christ refers to John the Baptist as: *"He was a burning and shining lamp, and you were willing to rejoice for a while in his light."*

> *He was a burning and shining lamp, and you were willing to rejoice for a while in his light. But the testimony that I have is greater than that of John. For the works that the Father has given me to accomplish, the very works that I am doing, bear witness about me that the Father has sent me. John 5:35-36*

John was a great source of light, but his time ended with Christ's appearance. Christ's teachings supersede all that John the Baptist preached. Christ is The Light of the World. His light is a new light for a new age. The time has come to put the old behind us. The old ways did not give us peace and tranquility nor did they show us the way to an abundant spiritual life. We need a fresh start with new teachings that stem from light that has the intensity to dispel the darkness that has engulfed our world for so long. This light is the light of Christ buried deep within us. It is time to wake it up and be guided by it.

Keep in mind that the light Christ is referring to is not the simple light from a lamp for there are two types of light—physical and spiritual. The source of physical light is the lamp, the candle, the bulb, the match, the fire and ultimately, the sun. The source of inner spiritual light is our conscience, The Voice Within, and the Inner Spiritual Self or the Kingdom of God Within.

Physical light dispels physical darkness. Spiritual light is divine light. It dispels ignorance, fear and superstition. When Christ declared that He was "The Light of the World", He affirmed the presence of divinity. When He said, "I am with you, always", He asserted that this divine light is within us, always. It is ready to shine if we allow it and not hide it under a "basket."

Personalizing the Parable

We have a divine light within us. It is our Inner Spiritual Self. This light is dim in most people. Like Aladdin's magical lamp, it must be rubbed, polished, nurtured and fanned to allow its brilliance to shine forth. As we grow and mature spiritually, we become a lighthouse constantly shining our inner light as our aura, a beacon that suffuses love, joy and compassion.

If our inner light shines brightly, we demonstrate the presence of the divine light within us. We never hide our light because we are fearless. We never give the forces of evil and darkness a chance because we are always vigilant. We live moral, principle-based lives. We live and speak our truth. We see clearly. We hear distinctly and our hearts are full of love, empathy and understanding. We do not judge. We do not favor one against another. We become peacemakers and we are known as Children of God.

We have an internal "lamp" that will guide us if we learn how to use it. Once awakened, it will shine brightly at important junctures in our lives. It will communicate with us as an inspiration, a strong feeling, an intuition or it will thunder forth as an inner knowing. Our "lamp" will not show us the grand plan for our lives, only the next step we need to take. Our "lamp's" light extends only to our immediate environment and that is where we can make a difference.

The light of our lamp comes from three sources that must work together: Mind, Heart and the Inner Spiritual Self. For our light to shine brighter, these must be our priority to cultivate.

Why the Parable?

- We are the light of the world. We must never forget this!
- We light the path of another's life by being a light ourselves.
- Others will feel our light and they will be impacted.
- Light exposes what the dark hides.
- A laser focused light is required to reveal dark hidden secrets.

- We must be selective in what we see, hear and believe.
- The brighter we shine our light, the faster we will grow spiritually.
- The eyes are the lamp of the body. We must learn what to focus on and what to ignore.
- Our eyes are "bad" when we focus on negativity.
- Our eyes are "healthy" when we see and praise the good in others.
- John the Baptist symbolized the end of an era, the Old.
- Christ is the shining light of the world. He is the beginning of a New Era.
- An unlit lamp is useless regardless of where we place it.
- We must continuously fan the flame of our fire so our light shines brightly.
- The fuel of our lamp is zeal, enthusiasm and purity of heart.

The Parable from Other sources

Gospel of Mark
A Lamp Under a Basket
And he said to them, "Is a lamp brought in to be put under a basket, or under a bed, and not on a stand? For nothing is hidden except to be made manifest; nor is anything secret except to come to light. If anyone has ears to hear, let him hear." And he said to them, "Pay attention to what you hear: with the measure you use, it will be measured to you, and still more will be added to you. For to the one who has, more will be given, and from the one who has not, even what he has will be taken away." Mark 4: 21-25

Gospel of Luke
A Lamp Under a Jar
"No one after lighting a lamp covers it with a jar or puts it

under a bed, but puts it on a stand, so that those who enter may see the light. For nothing is hidden that will not be made manifest, nor is anything secret that will not be known and come to light. Take care then how you hear, for to the one who has, more will be given, and from the one who has not, even what he thinks that he has will be taken away." Luke 6:16-18

The Light in You

"No one after lighting a lamp puts it in a cellar or under a basket, but on a stand, so that those who enter may see the light. Your eye is the lamp of your body. When your eye is healthy, your whole body is full of light, but when it is bad, your body is full of darkness. Therefore be careful lest the light in you be darkness. If then your whole body is full of light, having no part dark, it will be wholly bright, as when a lamp with its rays gives you light." Luke 11: 33-36

Gospel of Thomas

What you hear with your ear, preach in other's ears from your housetops. For no one lights a lamp and puts it under a bushel, nor does he put it in a hidden place. Instead, he sets it on a lampstand so that everyone who comes in and out can see its light. (saying # 33)

PARABLE OF THE SPECK AND THE LOG

Everything that irritates us about others can lead us to an understanding of ourselves. —Carl Jung

The Parables

"Judge not, that you be not judged. For with the judgment you pronounce you will be judged, and with the measure you use it will be measured to you. Why do you see the speck that is in your brother's eye, but do not notice the log that is in your own eye? Or how can you say to your brother, 'Let me take the speck out of your eye,' when there is the log in your own eye? You hypocrite, first take the log out of your own eye, and then you will see clearly to take the speck out of your brother's eye." Matt 7:1-5

He also told them a parable: "Can a blind man lead a blind man? Will they not both fall into a pit? A disciple is not above his teacher, but everyone when he is fully trained will be like his teacher. Why do you see the speck that is in your brother's eye, but do not notice the log that is in your own eye? How can you say to your brother, 'Brother, let me take out the speck that is in your eye,' when you yourself do not see the log that is in your own eye? You hypocrite, first take the log out of your own eye, and then you will see clearly to take out the speck that is in your brother's eye.

Luke 6:39-42

The Hidden Meaning

We all have logs in our eyes for we have eyes, but we cannot see. We also have wax in our ears for we have ears, but we cannot hear. Our hearts are hardened like rocks. We go to war and we kill thousands, perhaps even hundreds of thousands of people and we are OK with that for "they" are the "enemy." We have judged them to be so. They could just as easily have been our brothers, sisters, neighbors, friends and family. We emphasize differences. We overlook how similar we really are.

We are not born with logs in our eyes. We acquire our logs over time. Initially, it is only a speck. Over time, it grows into a log and we become deaf and blind to the humanity within us and in others.

A speck and a log are akin to sin. The eyes are analogous to the heart. We are not born in original sin or with any other sin. Mostly, we are conceived and born in love. It is our culture, upbringing, beliefs, and philosophies of life that desensitize us. We lose our humanity. Our speck, over time, becomes a log.

Some believe that they are better than others. They deserve all the good life has to offer. Deep down, they might even believe that "they are the chosen" with all the privileges that go with it including denying basic human rights to the less fortunate.

Some who are powerful use their power to impose their will on the less privileged. Their ego is always inflated. They are right and everyone else is wrong. They have the answers and everyone should listen to them. These are the logs that blind. They are eager to point out the speck in someone else's eye, yet they are unaware of what blinds them. They live in glass houses, yet, they are the first to cast stones at others.

> *And as they continued to ask him, he stood up and said to them, "Let him who is without sin among you be the first*

to throw a stone at her." John 8:7

When we have a log in our eyes, we do not see the other person. Worse yet, we do not see ourselves. We do not feel the impact of our actions on others.

A log is a multiplicity of fibers. What we have is not one large item. It can be, but most likely what we have are several items bundled together forming a thick log. These must be untangled and removed, one by one.

And what constitutes our log?

- Ignorance
- Bias
- Jealousy
- Prejudice
- Hatred
- Pride
- Deep seated envy and many other vices

And what is the speck in someone else's eye? A trivial irritant, perhaps more to us than the person who has the speck.

How to get rid of the log in our eyes

Christ showed us through parable and example how to remove the logs from our eyes. We do this by following the example set by Christ. Instead of 12 disciples, we must have 12 disciplines that we work on—6 virtues we choose to cultivate and 6 vices we choose to eradicate.

It is incredible that Christ, being the teacher, tells us that we can be like Him if we apply ourselves, work on our deficiencies, and perfect our character and personality. The more spiritual we become, the more Christlike we are in our conduct and abilities.

> *A disciple is not above his teacher, but everyone when he is fully trained will be like his teacher. Luke 6:40*

The blind leading the blind

"Can a blind man lead a blind man? Will they not both fall into a pit?"

Unfortunately, many who lead us, though they may be sincere, are spiritually blind. They cannot lead us to any "promised land". If we follow blind leaders, we will stumble. We will lose our way. If we decide to follow, it is best to have leaders whose eyes are wide open so they can see clearly and lead. Leaders whose ears are clear so they can hear and understand and whose hearts are pliable and compassionate so they can feel and empathize. The best leader to follow resides within us as our Inner Spiritual Self.

Very few are physically blind, but most of us are spiritually blind. By cultivating our virtues and by eradicating our vices, we become more spiritual. Our eyes open; our ears clear; our hearts soften; we begin to see, hear and feel; we become compassionate. By working on ourselves, we stop scrutinizing others and we become less judgmental.

Personalizing the Parable

We are not here to change the world. We are here to work on ourselves. We can be better and we should constantly strive to improve. The best way to influence others is by example. Actions speak louder than words. Most start life with one "speck", some with two and a few with five. We are expected to eliminate our "specks" and not allow them to grow into logs. We should invest in ourselves. We can continuously cultivate our minds by what we read, how we think and the habits we form. We can take better care of our bodies, refine our emotions and deepen our relationships especially with loved ones. We have a lot of work to do on ourselves. It is much easier to find our way around if we have no specks in our eyes and we can see clearly.

If we live in glass houses, we should not throw stones at others. Judging others indicates that we know better. But do we? Even if we do, are we helping others by judging them? Instead of judging others, we should have empathy and compassion because we have been there and we understand. Perhaps we can lend a helping hand instead. Better yet, instead of focusing on others, let us work on ourselves. Our example is the best way we can influence others.

Ironically, many who have suffered have no qualms inflicting ten times more suffering on others less fortunate than themselves. Might does not make right. What goes around comes around. How we treat others matters for there are spiritual laws in place to ensure that. Karma is one such law. That is why Christ stated:

> "Judge not, that you be not judged. For with the judgment you pronounce you will be judged, and with the measure you use it will be measured to you." Matt 7:1-2

> "Judge not, and you will not be judged; condemn not, and you will not be condemned; forgive, and you will be forgiven; give, and it will be given to you. Good measure, pressed down, shaken together, running over, will be put into your lap. For with the measure you use it will be measured back to you." Luke 6:37-38

Refraining from judgment is a virtue. The easiest way to accomplish that is to shift the focus from others to self.

How we treat others comes back to us multiplied. The seeds we plant reproduce according to their nature. Sowing seeds of goodwill transforms our lives into a beautiful orchard. Sowing seeds of malice will result in a life as desolate as a desert.

Why the Parable?

- We need to focus on ourselves.
- We must constantly strive to be better.
- We can choose 6 virtues to cultivate.
- We can select 6 vices to eradicate.
- We cannot see ourselves or others clearly as long we have a log in our eyes.
- The speck in someone else's eye is perhaps more of an irritant to us than to them. We should ignore it.
- Everyone has something in their eyes. No one is perfect. We cannot see what is in another's eye, unless we first clear what is in ours.
- Many of our leaders have logs in their eyes. They are blind. We need not follow them. Instead, we should focus on what we need to do to remove our blinders and see clearly.
- There is hope for us. We, the students, can be like Christ, the teacher, if we apply ourselves.

The Parable from Other Sources

Gospel of Thomas

You see the splinter in your brother's eye but you do not see the plank in your own eye. When you have taken the plank out of your own eye, then you will be able to see and remove the splinter from your brother's eye. (saying 26)

If a blind man leads a blind man, both of them will fall into a ditch. (saying #34)

PARABLE OF THE NEW CLOTH ON AN OLD GARMENT

If you want something new, you have to stop doing something old. —Peter Drucker

The Parable

No one puts a piece of unshrunk cloth on an old garment, for the patch tears away from the garment, and a worse tear is made. Neither is new wine put into old wineskins. If it is, the skins burst and the wine is spilled and the skins are destroyed. But new wine is put into fresh wineskins, and so both are preserved." Matt 9:16-17

The Hidden Meaning

Christ could not speak His mind and offer His teachings plainly and openly. Even by hiding His teachings in parables, He still ended up being tried, persecuted and crucified. Christ did not teach openly, not just because people could not understand, but because of what they would do to Him—murder Him before He could complete His mission.

This parable is one of the simplest to understand, yet it hides a deeper meaning fundamental to the core message of Christ. To understand the hidden meaning in this parable and to know the secret hidden within it, we must have eyes that see, ears that hear and hearts that feel. We must not be prejudiced or biased. We must be fearlessly interested in understanding and knowing.

The Old garment and wineskin are the Old teachings and the Law. The New cloth and wineskin are the New teachings and Grace. What Christ is revealing in this parable is His desire to move us away from the Old to the New, from the Law to Grace and from religion to spirituality.

Items that coexist must match, old with old; new with new; shrunk cloth with shrunk garment; old wine in old wineskin and new wine in new wineskin. Christ and His teachings are the new. John the Baptist and the Old Testament are the Old. Christ's teachings should not be mixed with or confused with the Old teachings which represent the Law.

Wine had a special significance to the ancients. Wine is the transformation of the grape juice into a potent brew which transforms those who imbibe it. Wine is a symbolic representation of blood, the carrier of the Life Force. It signifies transformation.

Garments are what we cover ourselves with. In this case, physical garments are the clothes we wear, intellectual garments are our beliefs, and spiritual garments are our faith and philosophy of life.

Christ wants us to shed the Old and adopt the New. He is making everything new.

> And he who was seated on the throne said, "Behold, I am making all things new." Also he said, "Write this down, for these words are trustworthy and true." *Rev 21:5*

Let us now consider the distinction between religion, history and spirituality.

Religion

Religion is a belief in a superhuman power or powers, and the worship of a deity or deities. According to Wikipedia:

> *Religion is a range of* social-cultural systems, *including designated* behaviors *and practices,* morals, beliefs, worldviews, texts, sanctified places, prophecies, ethics, or organizations, *that generally relate humanity to* supernatural, transcendental, *and* spiritual *elements—although there is no scholarly consensus over what precisely constitutes a religion. Different religions may or may not contain various elements ranging from the* divine, sacredness, faith, *and a supernatural being or beings.*

Religion is a belief system. It is not history nor does it have to be based on facts or truth. Anyone is allowed to believe whatever they like. There does not have to be agreement between various groups of people as to what constitutes truth. Religion is belief and faith without needing proof. Various groups can have opposing beliefs and live harmoniously together.

History

According to Wikipedia:

> *History 'inquiry; knowledge acquired by investigation' is the systematic study and documentation of the human* past. *History is an* academic discipline *that uses a* narrative *to describe, examine, question, and analyse past events, and investigate their patterns of cause and effect. Historians debate which narrative best explains an event, as well as the significance of different causes and effects. Historians debate the* nature of history *as an end in itself, and its usefulness in giving perspective on the problems of the present.*

History is not a belief system. It is evidence based. Historians can investigate past evidence and arrive at conclusions. Historians can discuss history and reach differing conclusions, but they cannot dispute the evidence itself. This evidence is available to all to investigate. Historians use scientific tools and techniques to arrive at their conclusions.

Spirituality

Spirituality is the knowledge that we are more than the physical body and that within us is a spark of divinity. This spark is the Inner Spiritual Self that Christ refers to as the Kingdom of God within. We are here to cultivate it. It is the "lamp within" that must be lit and placed on the "mountain top" for all to see.

Spirituality entails discovering and nurturing the spark, variously called: the "yeast", the "seed," the "pearl", the "treasure" and the "net" within. Spirituality does not call for any intermediaries between us and the divine. There are several paths to discover and nurture the light within. Each individual can choose and follow the path that is most appealing. Each individual can even make up his or her own unique path.

The focus of spirituality is spiritual truths, not historical facts or religious beliefs. Spiritual seekers look for ways to further their understanding of the spiritual world in any and all systems. They are not limited to one source for facts. They dig deep for the hidden meaning buried in parables, symbols and allegories. Their main focus is learning, spiritual growth and perfecting their character and personality. Spiritual seekers are on a path to discover how to be Christlike in temperament and in action.

What is important for spiritual seekers is not holy books. Books are written by individuals using words which can be misunderstood, mistranslated or tampered with. While religion emphasizes holy books as the Word of God, spiritual seekers place their importance on the Work of God—human beings and nature. These are the two books that spiritual seekers study.

Personalizing the Parable

Our beliefs must match and harmoniously coexist. We must be true to ourselves with no patching of mismatched and conflicting beliefs. We must be pure, single-minded and unequivocal. We cannot put our hands to the "plow" and look back.

> *Jesus said to him, "No one who puts his hand to the plow and looks back is fit for the kingdom of God." Luke 9:62*

The plow is the decision to follow Christ's teachings. Once we adopt Christ's teachings, we cannot look back. We must keep our gaze forward.

We cannot adopt two conflicting systems of belief. Within us, there is only one master and that is our budding Christ Consciousness, our Inner Spiritual Self. This inner self is the one we must heed. Christ represents the new garment and the new wine. The old rules, regulations, commandments and edicts are old cloths. They are unfit to be patched with the new teachings of Christ.

The inner self in most people is the ego. It is of "base metal" such as tin or lead. The ego is selfish and concerned with survival, status and wealth. It must be transformed into the spiritual self, the "noble metals" of gold and platinum. Our life is meant to transmute the base into the noble, our vices into virtues and our selfish ego into the altruistic spiritual self. That is why the first miracle Christ performed was the changing of water, a common liquid, into wine, the essence of our life force. He was showing us the purpose of life—transmuting the ordinary into the extraordinary, water into wine.

> *Now there were six stone water jars there for the Jewish rites of purification, each holding twenty or thirty gallons. Jesus said to the servants, "Fill the jars with*

water." And they filled them up to the brim. And he said to them, "Now draw some out and take it to the master of the feast." So they took it. When the master of the feast tasted the water now become wine, and did not know where it came from (though the servants who had drawn the water knew), the master of the feast called the bridegroom and said to him, "Everyone serves the good wine first, and when people have drunk freely, then the poor wine. But you have kept the good wine until now." This, the first of his signs, Jesus did at Cana in Galilee, and manifested his glory. And his disciples believed in him. John 2:6-11

The teachings of Christ are the good wine served last. It is all we need to live happy, fulfilled and productive lives.

Why the Parable?

This is one of the most important parables to understand.

We are brought up to accept that the New teachings of Christ complement or are a continuation of the Old. This is completely against what Christ is telling us in this parable as He also did on several other occasions. In fact, the Old and the New are on opposite ends of a spectrum. The Old is based on laws and commandments that control and regulate every aspect of our lives. Obedience is the basis of the Old and severe punishment follows for those who break the law. The Old Testament is violent containing some of the worst atrocities committed against innocent people. Murder, destruction and even genocides are rampant. The New Testament is the polar opposite. It is the Good News that is meant to set us free from these laws and regulations by emphasizing the one law of love. Christ is gentle, compassionate, caring and loving. While the Old is judgmental, the New does not judge. While the Old is for a select group of people (The Chosen), the New accepts all races, genders and nationalities.

Christ's message is unique based on love and service. Christianity is the New cloth, the New Wine and it cannot be mixed with the Old cloth or put in Old Wineskins. Unfortunately, that is exactly where Christianity stands now. It has mistakenly annexed the two. It has patched the new cloth with the old garment and put the new wine in old wineskin. This has to end. Christianity must be pure and stand on its own merits.

Christ is not the Messiah. He was not a military leader set on freeing the people from foreign occupiers. Religious historians know better. They know that none of the prophesies in the Old Testament are about Jesus Christ, but rather, about contemporaries of the Old Testament. The prophets were prophesizing about events that would take place within a decade or less, not hundreds of years in the future. So why did the writers of the Gospels insert these assertions to imply that Christ is the Messiah?

The early Christian churches wanted to attract a diverse group of people into Christianity and the best way to do that was to show commonality between Christianity and the other belief systems. To appeal to the various sects and belief systems, they borrowed aspects from these systems that would induce these people to become Christians. To attract pagans, they incorporated pagan holidays and rituals. To attract Jews, they claimed that Jesus was their expected Messiah. To prove their case, they added to the New Testament phrases and acts to demonstrate that the prophesies of old were being fulfilled in Christ. This was not easy, so they manipulated the actions and statements of Christ to mirror these prophesies. This is easy to see once we remove the veil obstructing our vision and read the following passages with an open mind. We can easily see that they were manipulated to make their case. I will only list a couple here. For more examples, please refer to Appendix A.

> *Now all this was done, that it might be fulfilled which was spoken of the Lord by the prophet, saying, Behold, a virgin shall be with child, and shall bring forth a son, and they shall call his name Emmanuel, which being interpreted is, God with us. Matt 1:22-23*

This prophesy is in the New Testament. We are expected to believe that this is about Mary and Jesus. The following is the original prophecy from Issaiah:

> *Therefore the Lord himself will give you a sign. Behold, the virgin shall conceive and bear a son, and shall call his name Immanuel. He shall eat curds and honey when he knows how to refuse the evil and choose the good. For before the boy knows how to refuse the evil and choose the good, the land whose two kings you dread will be deserted. Isa 7:14-16*

Unless we read the context in which the prophecy was made, we can be easily fooled. From the above, we can see that Jesus's name was not Emmanuel and He did not eat curds and honey. Note the quote: *"For before the boy knows how to refuse the evil and choose the good, the land whose two kings you dread will be deserted."* In other words, this prophecy will be fulfilled before the boy knows how to refuse the evil and choose the good. This prophecy is about a land that has two kings. There were no two kings during the life of Jesus, but there were two kings around the time of the prophecy, one in Judea and the other in Israel.

Additionally, according to Professor Bart Ehrman, the word translated as "virgin", in the original Hebrew meant "a young woman."

Here is another prophecy:

> *And was there until the death of Herod: that it might be fulfilled which was spoken of the Lord by the prophet, saying,* **Out of Egypt have I called my son. Matt 2:15**

And here is the original prophecy:

When Israel was a child, then I loved him, and called my son out of Egypt. Hos 11:1

Reading the original prophecy, it is evident that the prophecy was not about Jesus. It was about Israel. But to make this prophecy about Jesus, Mary, Joseph and the child Jesus had to go to Egypt. There is no historical evidence this ever happened.

While Matthew mentions the flight to Egypt,

Now when they had departed, behold, an angel of the Lord appeared to Joseph in a dream and said, "Rise, take the child and his mother, and flee to Egypt, and remain there until I tell you, for Herod is about to search for the child, to destroy him." And he rose and took the child and his mother by night and departed to Egypt Matt 2:13-14

Luke makes it clear that this did not happen. Instead of going to Egypt, the family went to Jerusalem for the purification.

And at the end of eight days, when he was circumcised, he was called Jesus, the name given by the angel before he was conceived in the womb. And when the time came for their purification according to the Law of Moses, they brought him up to Jerusalem to present him to the Lord. Luke 2:20-21

A careful examination of these and the passages in Appendix A will clearly show that these insertions of prophesies are artificial. They are created to link Jesus to the expected Messiah. They are meant to attract followers by demonstrating that Christ was the Messiah they have been waiting for.

Individuals seeking spiritual growth care less about history or prophesies. They are only interested in the spiritual messages contained in the teachings and especially in the parables. Their aim is to discover how they can nurture the "seed" of spirituality within so it can grow into a magnificent "tree".

To sum up:

- Christ is the **new** wine. He is showing us a **new** way—the way to discover the Kingdom of Heaven within.
- Christ wants us to make a clean break with the Old.
- Christ uses the parable of the wine because wine is symbolic of transformation.
- To be transformed, we cannot mix new wine with the old or store our new wine in old wineskins. The teachings of Christ should be kept pure and pristine.
- The use of garments in the parable alludes to the teachings. He wants us to keep His teachings unpatched to old garments or old teachings.
- Each New Age is built on the ruins of the old. The old is for us to learn from so we can be better. It should not entrap and enslave us.
- With Christ, life is transformational. We learn to transform the ordinary into the extraordinary. We distill "wine" from everyday living.
- With Christ's parables and teachings, we have all we need to live an enlightened life.
- The parables of Christ are an excellent source for discovering spiritual truth. To glean these truths requires open-mindedness, courage and diligence.

The Parable from Other Sources

Gospel of Mark

No one sews a piece of unshrunk cloth on an old garment. If he does, the patch tears away from it, the new from the old, and a worse tear is made. And no one puts new wine into old wineskins. If he does, the wine will burst the skins

—and the wine is destroyed, and so are the skins. But new wine is for fresh wineskins." Mark 2:21-22

Gospel of Thomas

It is impossible for a man to mount two horses or draw two bows. A servant cannot serve two masters; he will honor the one and scorn the other. No one drinks vintage wine and immediately wants to drink new wine. New wine is not put into old wine skins, for they might burst; and vintage wine is not poured into new wine skins, because it might spoil. No one sews an old patch on to a new garment, for it will tear. (saying #47)

PARABLE OF THE DIVIDED KINGDOM

He who does not see the angels and devils in the beauty and malice of life will be far removed from knowledge, and his spirit will be empty of affection. — Khalil Gibran

The Parable

But when the Pharisees heard this, they said, "It is only by Beelzebub, the prince of demons, that this fellow drives out demons." Jesus knew their thoughts and said to them, "Every kingdom divided against itself will be ruined, and every city or household divided against itself will not stand. If Satan drives out Satan, he is divided against himself. How then can his kingdom stand? And if I drive out demons by Beelzebub, by whom do your people drive them out? So then, they will be your judges. But if it is by the Spirit of God that I drive out demons, then the kingdom of God has come upon you. "Or again, how can anyone enter a strong man's house and carry off his possessions unless he first ties up the strong man? Then he can plunder his house. "Whoever is not with me is against me, and whoever does not gather with me scatters. Matt 12:24-30

The Hidden Meaning

For a very long time people have been attempting to explain evil. It started in the proverbial Garden of Eden when, supposedly, the serpent tempted Eve. After that, the serpent became synonymous with the Devil and evil.

We must distinguish natural calamities from evil acts. Hurricanes, tornadoes, earthquakes, floods and fires are not evil. They are natural events. Evil is when there is an intent to harm. In other words, only humans can be evil. Evil is with us today in the hearts and intentions of people who do harm. Those who carry out evil acts are ego-driven, selfish and immature. Evil doers can be individuals or nations, ordinary people or even presidents of countries.

Christ's intention was to serve, to heal and to love. His acts can never be considered evil. The Pharisees accused Christ of driving out evil spirits by the power of evil to justify their refusal to accept Christ as a messenger of God.

Most believe that there are two "kingdoms", God and Satan, good and evil. These two are **allegories**. God is the ultimate good and Satan is the ultimate evil. These are not physical entities. They are tendencies in the hearts and minds of individuals. They are the opposite ends of the same continuum, different only in their consequences.

Not only is the "Kingdom of God" within us, so is the "Kingdom of Satan". These exist in individuals as germ seeds. If we dwell on, activate and exemplify the "Kingdom of God" within us, we express Godliness. If, on the other hand, we dwell on, activate and exemplify the "Kingdom of Satan" within us, we do evil deeds and express Satan in our evil acts.

We know that the kingdoms of God and Satan are allegories because they are presented so in the Bible. Good and evil spirits are presented as forces that act on people to impel them to act one way or the other. We must choose between the two. It is our choice and action that determines the nature of an activity as good or evil. God and the Devil are not adversaries. Allegorical Satan provides the opportunity for humans to be tested just as Jesus was tested. If we are not tested, we do not know where we stand, how much we have progressed or where our weaknesses are. When Jesus was tested, He triumphed and His fully developed spirituality shone forth. When we are tested, we often give in to temptation and succumb to temporary pleasures at the expense of spiritual pleasures that endure.

We can clearly see that Satan and God are not adversaries from the example of Job. Job was tested as an agreement between God and Satan. In fact, it was a wager between the two of them.

> *Now there was a day when the sons of God came to present themselves before the LORD, and Satan also came among them. The LORD said to Satan, "From where have you come?" Satan answered the LORD and said, "From going to and fro on the earth, and from walking up and down on it." And the LORD said to Satan, "Have you considered my servant Job, that there is none like him on the earth, a blameless and upright man, who fears God and turns away from evil?" Then Satan answered the LORD and said, "Does Job fear God for no reason? Have you not put a hedge around him and his house and all that he has, on every side? You have blessed the work of his hands, and his possessions have increased in the land. But stretch out your hand and touch all that he has, and he will curse you to your face." And the LORD said to Satan, "Behold, all that he has is in your hand. Only against him do not stretch out your hand." So Satan went out from the presence of the LORD. Job 1:6-12*

A kingdom divided against itself cannot stand

> *"Every kingdom divided against itself will be ruined, and every city or household divided against itself will not stand."* Matt 12:25

Divided nations, societies and households are weak, easily controlled, manipulated and ruled over. United nations, societies and households are strong, invincible and prosperous. Division leads to strife, conflict and ruin. Union results in peace, cooperation and abundance.

It was the practice of the colonial powers to divide so they could conquer and rule over other nations. Keeping nations divided and warring among themselves makes them easy prey to outside manipulation and control. The strongest nations on the planet are those composed of smaller units united into a larger whole—The United States of America, the European Union and China. The future of the planet depends on which way nations proceed. Forging unions such as The United African Nations, United Middle East and United South America will result in affluence, peace and abundance for all. Remaining divided and warring will keep these nations poor, weak and struggling.

Christ's advice: *"Every kingdom divided against itself will be ruined, and every city or household divided against itself will not stand"* is poignant and timely. Christ uniquely instructed us to "love our enemies". In other words, to avoid having enemies. This is not as difficult as it seems. We can challenge each other without being mean spirited. We can compete without feeling enmity. The purpose of competition is improvement in both competing parties.

Only ego-driven individuals and nations can have enemies. Spiritual beings never have enemies because they see others as themselves. Christ did not have enemies. Others considered Christ to be an enemy because they did not like what He stood for. Christ, however, never looked at anyone as an enemy, even those who persecuted and crucified Him. He simply forgave them *"for they know not what they do."*

If a divided house leads to ruin, then a united house leads to wonderful achievements. There is nothing more productive than joint ventures between individuals and nations. Cooperation is the name of the game. It is far more productive than destructive divisions.

Personalizing the Parable

There is evil in the world. This evil does not exist in spirits, Beelzebub or the Devil, but rather in the minds and hearts of people. Evil is a sign of immaturity and low spiritual development. Acting selfishly, causing harm, pain and suffering to others is mean-spirited and evil. Functioning from our egos, believing in "survival of the fittest" and caring only for our interests is evil. Functioning from the Inner Spiritual Self results in compassionate, caring and empowering acts.

We must understand and fully accept that we are the creators of good and evil based on our thoughts, intentions, decisions and actions. We cannot exercise free will while functioning from our ego. The ego is governed by our accumulated habits, memories and tendencies of self-preservation and competition for survival. We can only exercise choice when we detach from the ego and function from our Inner Spiritual Self. Then we see others as human beings just like us. We have compassion and we act with respect, kindness and appreciation.

It is easy for the wolf to don sheep's clothing and fool us. Unless we are vigilant, fearless and functioning from our Inner Spiritual Self, we can be fooled. The Devil or Satan can appear as "the good guy" when in fact he is pure evil. Therefore, we must be gentle as doves and wise as serpents. Our eyes must always be open.

> *Behold, I send you forth as sheep in the midst of wolves: be ye therefore wise as serpents, and harmless as doves. Matt 10:16*

We are going to be tempted, tested and accused of a variety of evils when we shine our light. Shining our light on the dark reveals what the dark is hiding. We must have courage and be steadfast in serving the good. If we do not give in to temptation and are ready for every test, then there is nothing to fear. Guided by our inner spiritual light, our house will always remain united. We will be indomitable and our light will shine brightly and dispel the darkness. Darkness has no power over light.

Why the Parable?

Who is Beelzebub?

He is "Lord of the Flies". A god of Ekron in Philistia.

> *And Ahaziah fell down through a lattice in his upper chamber that was in Samaria, and was sick: and he sent messengers, and said unto them, Go, enquire of Baalzebub the god of Ekron whether I shall recover of this disease. 2Kgs 1:2*

The Pharisees called Beelzebub "Prince of the devils" because he could cure people possessed by lesser devils.

What are demons?

According to Barbara Walker author of **The Women's Encyclopedia of Myths and Secrets,** the word demon is derived from the Greek daimon, a personal spirit or a guardian angel. The church claims that demons were rebellious angels who fell with Lucifer.

Who is Satan?

According to Barbara Walker, early Egyptians called him The Great Serpent Sata. This is why in Revelations Satan is referred to as the Dragon. To the Hebrews, Satan was the adversary; one who tested the faith of another by asking tricky questions or posing problems to be solved.

Who is the Devil?

According to Barbara Walker, the words "devil" and "divinity" grew from the same root, Indo-European *devi* (Goddess) or *deva* (God), which became *daeva* (devil) in Persian.

What are the unclean spirits?

Unclean spirts were most probably mental and spiritual issues that tormented the individual.

How does healing take place?

Christ could heal because the patients believed in Him and had faith that they could be cured. They asked to be healed. Asking is seeking, which is very important. Christ had an incredible spiritual power that could infuse individuals and cleanse them of all impurities of mind and body.

Why challenge Christ's authority to heal?

It is shocking that when people see healing taking place and instead of marveling at the miracle of healing, they instead question the power behind it. The healing should be good enough as a testament of the intentions of the healer. Healing stems from compassion, caring and love. These are noble sources of spiritual power.

We are accustomed to attribute all evil to Beelzebub, demons, Satan, the Devil and to unclean spirits. None of these exist outside of ourselves. They are forces residing within us. Evil requires intent and only humans are endowed with intention. We must stop attributing our own evil acts to outside forces. These forces are within us. As long as we are ego-driven, we will commit evil. Once we rise above our ego and function from our Inner Spiritual Self, then there will be no more evil.

The serpent is not evil or the devil. If we cannot realize that a "talking" serpent in the Garden of Eden was meant to be symbolic, then we have a long way to go before we can wake up and become spiritually mature. The serpent represents desire stemming from our own thoughts and intentions. "Seeing something as good and desirable to "eat" is what leads us to act. Our actions have consequences which can be good or evil. Eve wanted to eat of the fruit of the tree because she desired knowledge. There is nothing wrong with that. What is wrong is when desire runs our lives and leads us to ruin. We must learn to manage our desires to make sure that they are noble and will not harm anyone. We cannot lust, be greedy, or take advantage of anyone. Desires are not evil. Uncontrolled and unmanaged desires often lead to evil acts. Uncontrolled desires are the unclean spirits within us. They need to be purged.

The Parable from Other Sources
Gospel of Mark

So Jesus called them over to him and began to speak to them in parables: "How can Satan drive out Satan? If a kingdom is divided against itself, that kingdom cannot stand. If a house is divided against itself, that house cannot stand. And if Satan opposes himself and is divided, he cannot stand; his end has come. In fact, no one can enter a strong man's house without first tying him up. Then he can plunder the strong man's house. Mark 3:23-27

PARABLE OF THE SOWER

It is not always granted to the sower to see the harvest. — Albert Schweitzer

The Parable

That same day Jesus went out of the house and sat beside the sea. And great crowds gathered about him, so that he got into a boat and sat down. And the whole crowd stood on the beach. And he told them many things in parables, saying: "A sower went out to sow. And as he sowed, some seeds fell along the path, and the birds came and devoured them. Other seeds fell on rocky ground, where they did not have much soil, and immediately they sprang up, since they had no depth of soil, but when the sun rose they were scorched. And since they had no root, they withered away. Other seeds fell among thorns, and the thorns grew up and choked them. Other seeds fell on good soil and produced grain, some a hundredfold, some sixty, some thirty. He who has ears, let him hear." Matt 13:1-9

The Hidden Meaning

Christ explains the hidden meaning of the parable of the Sower Himself.

And when he was alone, those around him with the twelve asked him about the parables. And he said to them, "To you has been given the secret of the kingdom of God, but for those outside everything is in parables, so that "they may indeed see but not perceive, and may indeed hear but not understand, lest they should turn and be forgiven."

And he said to them, "Do you not understand this parable? How then will you understand all the parables? The sower sows the word. And these are the ones along the path, where the word is sown: when they hear, Satan immediately comes and takes away the word that is sown in them. And these are the ones sown on rocky ground: the ones who, when they hear the word, immediately receive it with joy. And they have no root in themselves, but endure for a while; then, when tribulation or persecution arises on account of the word, immediately they fall away. And others are the ones sown among thorns. They are those who hear the word, but the cares of the world and the deceitfulness of riches and the desires for other things enter in and choke the word, and it proves unfruitful. But those that were sown on the good soil are the ones who hear the word and accept it and bear fruit, thirtyfold and sixtyfold and a hundredfold." Mark 4:10-20

"Hear then the parable of the sower: When anyone hears the word of the kingdom and does not understand it, the evil one comes and snatches away what has been sown in his heart. This is what was sown along the path. As for what was sown on rocky ground, this is the one who hears the word and immediately receives it with joy, yet he has no root in himself, but endures for a while, and when tribulation or persecution arises on account of the word, immediately he falls away. As for what was sown among thorns, this is the one who hears the word, but the cares of the world and the deceitfulness of riches choke the word, and it proves unfruitful. As for what was

sown on good soil, this is the one who hears the word and understands it. He indeed bears fruit and yields, in one case a hundredfold, in another sixty, and in another thirty." Matt 13:18-23

According to the parable, people must hear the "word" several times before it lands on fertile soil. In other words, seeds have four possible destinies before they fall into good soil and are fruitful.

Seeds falling along the path

Seeds falling along the path do not take hold, grow and yield results. This is because the path refers to individuals who are aimlessly walking the trail of life. These individuals are not focused on the spiritual. Even though they hear the "word", it does not sink in because they can be easily distracted. The birds that devour these seeds (*and the birds came and devoured them*) are the everyday distractions of life. These include financial worries, household chores, work and responsibilities.

> "when they hear, Satan immediately comes and takes away the word that is sown in them."

There is scarcely any time left for the serious matters of life. What free time these individuals have is used for drinking, socializing and entertainment. These are the "Satan" who takes away the seeds that are sown. Seeds falling along the path, get trod over and the "evil one or Satan" snatches them away.

The first few times people receive the "seeds", the soil is dry and inhospitable. Over several exposures, their "rock-hard" hearts and minds soften due to weathering and they become a bit more receptive.

Seeds that fall on rocky ground

> *"when they hear the word, immediately receive it with joy. And they have no root in themselves, but endure for a while; then, when tribulation or persecution arises on account of the word, immediately they fall away.*

Rocky ground has little moisture and soil. The second batch of seeds that fall on rocky ground find some soil and grow quickly but because the soil is shallow, they cannot establish deep roots. They perish swiftly from the scorching heat of the sun.

The rocky ground refers to individuals who are shallow. When they hear something new, they get excited and become eager to accept and embrace. However, as soon as they find anything they consider more important to do, they forget about what really matters. If someone challenges them about their newfound beliefs, they are unable to defend them and if they are offered something different, they accept it without questioning. When difficulties arise, they give up. Therefore, the teachings do not find fertile soil to establish roots and grow.

Seeds that are sown among thorns

> *They are those who hear the word, but the cares of the world and the deceitfulness of riches and the desires for other things enter in and choke the word, and it proves unfruitful.*

The third batch of seeds fall on prepared soil, but they are not alone. Surrounded by weeds and thorns, they choke and have no chance of blossoming. The thorns refer to individuals who are overwhelmed by cares and temptations. The seeds that fall on these individuals have to contend with uncontrolled desires and the pursuit of wealth.

For seeds to grow properly, they require nurturing. They need space, water and nutrients. If all they get are weeds competing with them, then they can suffocate. People who go to church once a week on Sundays and hear a great sermon that inspires them, forget about the sermon as soon as they get home. They have other things on their minds. There are sport games to watch, a golf game to play or visitors to entertain. It is the same story week after week. Time passes by and not much gets accomplished. What suffocates these people are the trivial affairs that consume their lives.

Seeds that fall on good soil

> *"But those that were sown on the good soil are the ones who hear the word and accept it and bear fruit, thirtyfold and sixtyfold and a hundredfold."*

Finally, individuals are ready to receive, accept and nurture the seeds. These seeds find a home, grow and produce an abundance of returns. The seeds that are sown in good soil take root and are fruitful, some thirty-fold, others sixty-fold and some one hundred-fold.

Most individuals with fertile soil are sincere, dedicated and serious. They want to learn, understand and know the truth. They desire spiritual growth. They want to make a difference in their lives and the lives of many. The seeds in these individuals are like yeast, a net, or a precious stone. They are put to great use. The teachings are valued and applied in their lives. Their growth is continuous. Their improvement is palpable. These individuals are the "salt" of the earth. They are the ones shining their "lamps" from the mountaintop. They listen to the Voice Within and are on an accelerated path to spirituality.

Personalizing the Parable

The seed is the word of God. This word of God is truth and the Good News. Christ is the Word of God as Logos. In other words, the hidden, secret teachings of Christ are the seeds that He scattered into the soil or minds of His listeners. Anyone reading the words of Christ should be looking for these seeds as gems hidden in the guise of parables.

The use of the words *"sown in his heart"* by Christ is significant. The words we hear end up in the mind. Unless they are entangled with the heart via emotions, they will not be anchored, produce roots, grow and be fruitful.

We too go through four stages when we encounter a new idea or a new truth.

In the first stage, when we first hear the truth, the words go in one ear and out of the other. We hear the words but we do not fully cognize the message. Unless we dwell on the meaning of what we hear, analyze it and think about it, it will not transfer from short-term memory to long-term memory and be anchored. When Christ says "evil ones or Satan" snatched the seeds away, He is referring to temptations that distract us and lead us off our intended path. The people in this category who do not comprehend the word are the ones Christ refers to as: *They have eyes, but they do not see. They have ears, but they do not hear.*

In the second stage, doubt, resistance and old beliefs prevent us from accepting the truth. These individuals hear the word but reject it outright. It does not jell with what they have been indoctrinated with. People in this group are set in their ways and it is very difficult to convince them of anything other than what they already know.

In the third stage, when individuals hear the "word", worldly cares, concerns and other priorities take center stage and the message is ignored. People in this group hear the word, accept it, but lack the necessary will to embody the new truth and live accordingly. They are the procrastinators. They will act, but always later, never now. "I will get serious and take action tomorrow, today I am kind of busy. There is always tomorrow to act".

In the fourth stage, when individuals hear the truth, they are excited because they recognize the truth. They accept it and incorporate it into their lives immediately. They are ready, prepared and willing to change their beliefs, ways and behaviors right away.

These individuals are committed to finding the truth. Based on their life experiences and in light of new knowledge, they know their views must be revised. They accept the new truth without any hesitancy.

Just as in the parable of the talents, the return on investment of time and effort depends solely on us. The benefits are immediate, but the measure of the yield is totally up to us. We can have a 30-fold return, a 60-fold return or even a 100-fold return. It depends on how serious we are, how engaged we are, and how committed we are to know the truth and to set ourselves free.

Why the Parable?

Who is the Sower?

God and Christ are meant to be the Sowers. However, these are not external forces. They reside within us. Hence, we are our own Sowers. We can sow in our minds and hearts via faith, intention, acceptance and purposeful action.

If we do not act to be our own Sower, others will gladly do it for us. We are bombarded daily by the media. They are trying to sow seeds in our minds. We can evaluate these "seeds", accept the good ones and reject the rest.

Where is the soil?

The soil is internal. It is our hearts and minds.

What is fertile soil?

A heart ready to embrace and a mind prepared to accept are fertile soils in which seeds will grow and yield an abundance.

What are the seeds?

Seeds are thoughts, words, feelings and intentions that we firmly plant in our minds and hearts through intentional and purposeful action.

What suffocates the seedling?

Doubt, fear, yielding to temptation, greed, procrastination, trials and tribulations.

What nurtures and fertilizes the seeds?

Faith, courage, acceptance, visualization, imagination, excitement, gratitude, joy and exhilaration.

A puzzling statement

> *And when he was alone, those around him with the twelve asked him about the parables. And he said to them, "To you has been given the secret of the kingdom of God, but for those outside everything is in parables, so that "they may indeed see but not perceive, and may indeed hear but not understand, lest they should turn and be forgiven." Mark 4:10-12*

Reading this statement can be puzzling indeed. *'so that "they may indeed see but not perceive, and may indeed hear but not understand, lest they should turn and be forgiven."*

Does Christ not want the people to see, understand and be forgiven? Of course He does but the people He is dealing with are the ones who have eyes, but cannot see, have ears, but cannot hear and have hearts, but cannot understand. If Christ taught these people plainly and openly saying what is on His mind and in His heart, they would stone Him on the spot and murder Him. He would die prematurely and be unable to complete His mission. Imagine Christ telling them to forget the prophets, to forget the old commandments, old rituals and practices and only love and serve. How would these stone-hearted people react? Even teaching through parables got Him in hot water. They still persecuted and crucified Him. These were not the right people to talk with openly and plainly. Christ was wise indeed to use parables to camouflage His message.

It is extremely difficult to communicate with those who refuse to see, hear and understand. They are the "swine" and we should not place our "pearls" before them.

> *"Do not give dogs what is holy, and do not throw your pearls before pigs, lest they trample them underfoot and turn to attack you". Matt 7:6*

The Parable from Other sources

Gospel of Mark

> *Again he began to teach beside the sea. And a very large crowd gathered about him, so that he got into a boat and sat in it on the sea, and the whole crowd was beside the sea on the land. And he was teaching them many things in parables, and in his teaching he said to them: "Listen! Behold, a sower went out to sow. And as he sowed, some seed fell along the path, and the birds came and devoured it. Other seed fell on rocky ground, where it did not have much soil, and immediately it sprang up, since it had no*

depth of soil. And when the sun rose, it was scorched, and since it had no root, it withered away. Other seed fell among thorns, and the thorns grew up and choked it, and it yielded no grain. And other seeds fell into good soil and produced grain, growing up and increasing and yielding thirtyfold and sixtyfold and a hundredfold." And he said, "He who has ears to hear, let him hear." Mark 4:1-9

Gospel of Luke

And when a great crowd was gathering and people from town after town came to him, he said in a parable, "A sower went out to sow his seed. And as he sowed, some fell along the path and was trampled underfoot, and the birds of the air devoured it. And some fell on the rock, and as it grew up, it withered away, because it had no moisture. And some fell among thorns, and the thorns grew up with it and choked it. And some fell into good soil and grew and yielded a hundredfold." As he said these things, he called out, "He who has ears to hear, let him hear." Luke 8:4-8

Gospel of Thomas

The Sower went out, filled his hand and sowed. Some seeds fell on the road; birds came and gathered them up. Others fell on the rock and did not take root in the earth and did not produce. Others fell among thorns; the thorns choked the seeds and worms ate them. But others fell on good ground and brought forth good fruit. These yielded sixty per measure and one hundred and twenty measures. (saying #9)

PARABLE OF THE WEEDS

The weeds keep multiplying in our garden, which is our mind ruled by fear. Rip them out and call them by name.
  —Sylvia Browne

The Parable

He put another parable before them, saying, "The kingdom of heaven may be compared to a man who sowed good seed in his field, but while his men were sleeping, his enemy came and sowed weeds among the wheat and went away. So when the plants came up and bore grain, then the weeds appeared also. And the servants of the master of the house came and said to him, 'Master, did you not sow good seed in your field? How then does it have weeds?' He said to them, 'An enemy has done this.' So the servants said to him, 'Then do you want us to go and gather them?' But he said, 'No, lest in gathering the weeds you root up the wheat along with them. Let both grow together until the harvest, and at harvest time I will tell the reapers, Gather the weeds first and bind them in bundles to be burned, but gather the wheat into my barn.'" Matt 13: 24-30

The Hidden Meaning

This is how Christ interprets this parable:

The Parable of the Weeds Explained

Then he left the crowds and went into the house. And his disciples came to him, saying, "Explain to us the parable of the weeds of the field." He answered, "The one who sows the good seed is the Son of Man. The field is the world, and the good seed is the sons of the kingdom. The weeds are the sons of the evil one, and the enemy who sowed them is the devil. The harvest is the end of the age, and the reapers are angels. Just as the weeds are gathered and burned with fire, so will it be at the end of the age. The Son of Man will send his angels, and they will gather out of his kingdom all causes of sin and all law-breakers, and throw them into the fiery furnace. In that place there will be weeping and gnashing of teeth. Then the righteous will shine like the sun in the kingdom of their Father. He who has ears, let him hear. Matt 13: 36-43

There are three levels to interpret this parable:

1. Simple, where a farmer plants good seeds and weeds grow among them.

2. Spiritual as Christ interpreted it.
   The field: the world.
   Good seeds: the Sons of the Kingdom, the spiritual people, the salt of the earth.
   Bad seeds: the Sons of evil. Evil doers. Anyone committing evil with or without knowledge.
   Weeds: the sons of the evil one—misguided people who have lost their way.
   Wheat: The teachings of Christ.

Sowers: Christ and the Devil.

The reapers: the angels. Angels are the messengers of God doing the will of the Father.

3. **Personal**

    The field: the mind, the heart and the world.

    Good seeds: good habits, attitudes, intentions, beliefs, actions and the words and teachings of Christ.

    Bad seeds: bad habits, negative attitudes, evil intentions, misguided beliefs and actions.

    Weeds: negative environment.

    Wheat: positive environment.

    Sowers: us and the media.

    The reapers: There are no actual reapers in life, only the consequences of our thoughts, intentions and actions. The results might be immediate or manifest later.

With this parable, Christ is explaining why we continue to have evil people in the world. Having evil people in our lives gives us the opportunity to confront them, stop them and neutralize their actions.

We need the challenges of evil so that our virtue may shine. By allowing evil people among us, their actions expose them and their intentions become manifest. They are no longer in hiding. In daylight, we can see them better and it becomes easier to confront them. With evil amongst us, we know what we must do. Our work is cut out for us.

Personalizing the Parable

We encounter weeds in three areas in our lives.

The first is the field of our minds and hearts. This is where bad thoughts, feelings, habits, attitudes, expectations and beliefs reside. This is where we must assume the role of the Sower. This is where we weed out the bad seeds and feed and nurture the good ones. The seeds here must be intentionally selected to serve us. Otherwise, they appear randomly as weeds. Since we are the Sower, we can carefully select the best seeds to plant in our minds and hearts.

Some of the worst weeds within us are negativity, fear and detrimental habits and beliefs.

The second field where we might encounter weeds is in our personal lives. These weeds cannot be plucked out and must be dealt with. These weeds can be physical challenges due to handicaps, mental or emotional scars that do not heal, or acrimonious relationships. The best way to deal with these weeds is to focus our attention elsewhere, away from them and into positive activities that we can engage in. Keep in mind that what we focus on we empower. We need to look away from our trials and gaze into greener pastures. By engaging in positive activities we minimize the impact of the negative. We can choose what to engage in, what thoughts we entertain and how we feel.

The third field is the world in which we exist and function. Here the weeds are the people we encounter, the books we read, the music and news we listen to and the activities we engage in. If these are not selected carefully, they can detrimentally impact the quality of our lives.

Weeds in general

Weeds are the negative elements in our lives such as doubt, insecurity, procrastination, jealousy, hate and the desire for revenge. They are our bad habits resulting from repeated bad thoughts, intentions and actions. Since these cannot be plucked and discarded, if they are not replaced by good habits, they can grow into shrubs, bushes and even trees. They become difficult to eradicate and can take over our lives.

At times we have no options but to confront evil people head-on. We do this with determination`, courage and with care and compassion.

Where do weeds come from?

Weeds are everywhere. They come through our media, culture, religious indoctrination, unquestioned beliefs and through imitation. Some weeds even appear in the guise of good seeds pretending to be wheat.

No one is free from weeds. No field is 100% wheat. As long as these weeds are few, manageable and do little harm, we can live with them. It behooves us to periodically examine our thoughts, intentions, actions and beliefs feeding the good "wheat", and "weeding out" the bad "weeds" by starving them. We can replace weeds with chosen seeds such as good thoughts, noble intentions, thought out actions and constructive beliefs.

While weeds appear in our lives in various forms, we are told that the good seeds are "wheat". Wheat is the staff of life; we make bread from it to sustain our lives. Christ is the bread of life. He was born in "Bethlehem"—house of bread in Syriac (Aramaic).

> *Jesus said to them, "I am the bread of life; whoever comes to me shall not hunger, and whoever believes in me shall never thirst. John 6:35*

What part of Christ is the good seeds? It is His words, message and teachings. These are seeds of "wheat" that fall into the soil of our minds and hearts. Most listeners let these seeds fall by the wayside and "birds" eat them up. Many have their hearts hardened like rock and cannot hear the message of Christ. Others have too many "thorns" within to accept anything new. A few have fertile minds and hearts. They accept Christ's message readily and become reborn anew.

While "wheat" seeds must be selected and planted, "weeds" grow naturally and without effort. Wheat is what we want.

We must choose it, plant it and nurture it until it grows and establishes a powerful root system. We do not want weeds. We cannot pluck them out and discard them for our weeds are bad thoughts, intentions, habits, beliefs, feelings and actions. The weeds within us grow alongside our good qualities. The only way we can get rid of our weeds is to **replace** them with good "wheat" seeds. By dwelling on and encouraging the good seeds, we ignore and starve the bad weeds.

To grow good "wheat" seeds into mature plants that yield manyfold returns, they must first be selected and buried in our minds and hearts and nurtured secretly for a long time before we see results.

> *Truly, truly, I say to you, unless a grain of wheat falls into the earth and dies, it remains alone; but if it dies, it bears much fruit. John 12:24*

Burying a seed until it dies so it bears much fruit means that we must create a good habit and, bury it deep within us, acting it out repeatedly until it becomes instinctual. Then it will bear much fruit. Seeds require a gestation period where they lie dormant or "dead" before they burst forth and we can see results.

Why the Parable

- We will always have some weeds in our lives.
- We are surrounded by weeds. The most stubborn ones are in our hearts and minds.
- The world will always harbor evildoers. They provide us the opportunity to confront them.
- We must remain vigilant against uninvited weeds.
- Weeds grow naturally and effortlessly.
- Seeds must be chosen, planted and nurtured (fertilized).
- We are bombarded by seeds continuously. Some are good seeds, most are not.
- We must be selective in what we allow to take root in our

minds and hearts.
- We should endeavor to be our own Sower of good seeds.
- We reap in accordance to the seeds we plant and nurture.
- What we dwell on, we empower. What we ignore will shrivel and die from lack of attention.
- If we neglect the garden of our lives, weeds will grow automatically. If allowed to grow rampant, they will take over our lives.

The Parable from Other Sources

Gospel of Thomas

The kingdom of the Father is like a man who had good seed. His enemy came by night and sowed weeds among the good seed. But the man did not let anyone pull up the weed. He said, "Do not do so because when you go to pull up the weed you pull up the wheat along with it." On the day of the harvest the weeds will be conspicuous; they will be pulled up and burned. (saying #57)

MYSTERY OF THE KINGDOM OF HEAVEN

What is the Kingdom of Heaven?

If the Kingdom of God is in you, you should leave a little bit of heaven wherever you go. —Cornel West

The Parables

Parable of the Mustard Seed

He put another parable before them, saying, "The kingdom of heaven is like a grain of mustard seed that a man took and sowed in his field. It is the smallest of all seeds, but when it has grown it is larger than all the garden plants and becomes a tree, so that the birds of the air come and make nests in its branches." Matt 13:31-32

Parable of the Leaven

He told them another parable. "The kingdom of heaven is like leaven that a woman took and hid in three measures of flour, till it was all leavened." Matt 13:33

Parable of the Hidden Treasure

"The kingdom of heaven is like treasure hidden in a field,

which a man found and covered up. Then in his joy he goes and sells all that he has and buys that field. Matt 13:44

Parable of the Pearl of Great Value

"Again, the kingdom of heaven is like a merchant in search of fine pearls, who, on finding one pearl of great value, went and sold all that he had and bought it. Matt 13:45-46

Parable of the Net

"Again, the kingdom of heaven is like a net that was thrown into the sea and gathered fish of every kind. When it was full, men drew it ashore and sat down and sorted the good into containers but threw away the bad. So it will be at the end of the age. The angels will come out and separate the evil from the righteous and throw them into the fiery furnace. In that place there will be weeping and gnashing of teeth. Matt 13:47-50

The Hidden Meaning

The concept of The Kingdom of Heaven was essential to Christ. He has many parables and references to this concept. This Kingdom of Heaven cannot be a physical kingdom where Christ returns and rules as a king. That is what the expected Messiah was supposed to do—return as a military king and free His people from the yoke of foreign occupation. Christ was anything but a military leader. He stated that His Kingdom was not earthly.

Jesus answered, "My kingdom is not of this world. If my kingdom were of this world, my servants would have been fighting, that I might not be delivered over to the Jews. But my kingdom is not from the world." John 18:36

The Kingdom of Heaven Christ was referring to was spiritual. He likened this kingdom to a seed, yeast, a treasure, a pearl of great value and to a net. To understand the hidden meaning of these allegories, we must keep in mind that Christ taught on three levels:

1. Publicly to those around Him
2. Via parables to future generations
3. Privately to His disciples.

1. What Christ Taught Publicly to Those Around Him

To pray in private, directly to Our Father;

But when you pray, go into your room and shut the door and pray to your Father who is in secret. And your Father who sees in secret will reward you. Matt 6:6

To be like children; pure, uncomplicated, innocent, inquisitive and playful;

And said, Verily I say unto you, Except ye be converted, and become as little children, ye shall not enter into the kingdom of heaven. Matt 18:3

To be humble, meek, and content;

Blessed are the poor in spirit, for theirs is the kingdom of heaven. Matt 5:3

To be proactive, not passive;

Ask, and it shall be given you; seek, and ye shall find; knock, and it shall be opened unto you: Matt 7:7

To not judge, to forgive, to not retaliate;

Judge not, that ye be not judged. Matt 7:1

To have faith;

Jesus turned, and seeing her he said, "Take heart, daughter; your faith has made you well." And instantly the woman was made well. Matt 9:22

Then he touched their eyes, saying, "According to your faith be it done to you." Matt 9:29

Then Jesus answered her, "O woman, great is your faith! Be it done for you as you desire." And her daughter was healed instantly. Matt 15:28

To love our neighbor, God, and even our enemies as we love ourselves.

The Great Commandment
And one of the scribes came up and heard them disputing with one another, and seeing that he answered them well, asked him, "Which commandment is the most important of all?" Jesus answered, "The most important is, 'Hear, O Israel: The Lord our God, the Lord is one. And you shall love the Lord your God with all your heart and with all your soul and with all your mind and with all your strength.' The second is this: 'You shall love your neighbor as yourself.' There is no other commandment greater than these." And the scribe said to him, "You are right, Teacher. You have truly said that he is one, and there is no other besides him. And to love him with all the heart and with all the understanding and with all the strength, and to love one's neighbor as oneself, is much more than all whole burnt offerings and sacrifices." And when Jesus saw that he answered wisely, he said to him, "You are not far from the kingdom

> of God." And after that no one dared to ask him any more questions. *Mark 12:28-34*

Christ's life was an example of what He taught. He never judged and never retaliated against those who judged, tortured and crucified Him. When Peter cut an ear off a guard, Christ reprimanded him and healed the man's ear.

> *And when those who were around him saw what would follow, they said, "Lord, shall we strike with the sword?" And one of them struck the servant of the high priest and cut off his right ear. But Jesus said, "No more of this!" And he touched his ear and healed him. Luke 22:49-51*

Christ's public teachings can be summed up in His Sermon on the Mount. *Matt. 5.*

2. What Christ Taught Via Parables to Future Generations

The core of Christ's hidden teachings reside in the parables. This book is dedicated to uncovering those secrets.

3. What Christ Taught Privately to His Disciples

- Who He was
- His Birth
- His Mission
- Why 12 Disciples?
- The Inner Self
- What exactly is the Kingdom of Heaven
- What Salvation Entails

Who He Was

He was someone who was very diligent studying, praying and meditating to have an understanding of His and God's nature.

Eventually, at the age of 30, while being baptized, the Holy Spirit (spiritual knowledge) descended on him and He knew. His eyes were opened and He was transformed from being The Son of Man into being The Son of God. He had received the Christ Consciousness.

His Birth

His mother was Mary and His father was Joseph. He had several brothers and sisters. Virgin birth does not allude to physical virginity. It refers to spiritual purity. There have been many virgin births throughout history. They mean the same thing—a pious, virtuous, healthy young woman giving birth to a special messenger.

Throughout the ages, world teachers have been born to help raise the consciousness of humanity. Christ was one of them. Many were born to virgins around December 25 to symbolize the birth of light. The sun descends and the days get shorter and shorter until December 21. This is the death of the light. For 3 days, the light (sun) stays in the same position in the sky at its lowest point. On December 25, the light, (sun) begins to rise again in the sky. Light is resurrected and is born anew. While the sun is symbolic of the physical light, Christ is symbolic of spiritual light—wisdom and understanding.

His Mission

Christ's mission was to bring light to the world by being light Himself and by living an exemplary life which He did. Christ never judged, retaliated or committed acts of violence against anybody. He was a living example of how we should be and how we should live. He was the torchbearer of a new cycle in the evolution of humanity. Did He succeed? Not on the massive scale we imagine. Most who call themselves Christians are not practicing Christianity. Anyone espousing unnecessary violence cannot be a follower of Christ.

We are falsely taught that Christ came as a fulfillment of Old Testament prophecies.

> *"Do not think that I have come to abolish the Law or the Prophets; I have not come to abolish them but to fulfill them. For truly, I say to you, until heaven and earth pass away, not an iota, not a dot, will pass from the Law until all is accomplished. Therefore whoever relaxes one of the least of these commandments and teaches others to do the same will be called least in the kingdom of heaven, but whoever does them and teaches them will be called great in the kingdom of heaven. For I tell you, unless your righteousness exceeds that of the scribes and Pharisees, you will never enter the kingdom of heaven. Matt 5:17-20*

Obviously, this cannot be an authentic saying of Christ. There are many statements attributed to Christ for the simple purpose of attracting Jews so they will convert to Christianity. By showing them that Christ is their anticipated Messiah and by inserting Old Testament prophecies in the New Testament, it was hoped to convince Jews to accept Jesus as their Messiah and convert. Similarly, by incorporating pagan rituals and holidays into Christianity, it was hoped to convert pagans into Christianity.

The life of Christ is the antithesis of the Old Testament. He did not live for "An eye for and eye." He did not enforce hundreds of commandments on His followers. He only gave them one commandment: Love everyone as yourself including your enemies. Unlike the Old Testament, Christ did not believe in enemies. He never went to war, hurt or harmed anyone. He never ordered the murder of anyone, let alone the murder of the first born of innocent people. He taught forgiveness. He healed as many as He could. He cleansed the unclean, gave sight to the blind, ability to walk to the lame, health for the sick. If anyone is interested in studying the difference between the concept of

God as Father taught by Christ and the god of the Old Testament, one need only study the book of Joshua and compare that to the teachings of "The Sermon on the Mount".

The end of the Old

> *Truly, I say to you, among those born of women there has arisen no one greater than John the Baptist. Yet the one who is least in the kingdom of heaven is greater than he. From the days of John the Baptist until now the kingdom of heaven has suffered violence, and the violent take it by force. For all the Prophets and the Law prophesied until John, and if you are willing to accept it, he is Elijah who is to come. He who has ears to hear, let him hear. Matt 11:11-15*

The above quote makes it crystal clear that the teachings of the Old Testament were for a time period until John the Baptist or until Christ was baptized. After that, it was the beginning of a new era, a new covenant, an age of enlightenment. From the above, even if we assume that when Christ said: *"I have not come to abolish them (the law) but to fulfill them"* it is evident that what He meant was that the laws served their purpose and we are done with them. For to fulfill is to achieve, to accomplish, to realize and to satisfy.

> *"The Law and the Prophets were until John; since then the good news of the kingdom of God is preached, and everyone forces his way into it. Luke 16:16*

The Law and the Prophesies end with John the Baptist. That is the Old. With Christ a new era begins, an era of spirituality—love, compassion, forgiveness, grace, acceptance of all and living together as one family with one God as our Father.

This becomes abundantly clear if we study His most explicit teaching—The Sermon on the Mount, where he repeatedly says:

> *"You have heard that it was said to those of old, 'You*

shall not murder; and whoever murders will be liable to judgment.' But I say to you that everyone who is angry with his brother will be liable to judgment; whoever insults his brother will be liable to the council; and whoever says, 'You fool!' will be liable to the hell of fire. Matt 5:21-22

"You have heard that it was said, 'You shall not commit adultery.' But I say to you that everyone who looks at a woman with lustful intent has already committed adultery with her in his heart. Matt 5:27-28

"Again you have heard that it was said to those of old, 'You shall not swear falsely, but shall perform to the Lord what you have sworn.' But I say to you, Do not take an oath at all, either by heaven, for it is the throne of God, or by the earth, for it is his footstool, or by Jerusalem, for it is the city of the great King. And do not take an oath by your head, for you cannot make one hair white or black. Let what you say be simply 'Yes' or 'No'; anything more than this comes from evil.7 Matt 5:33-37

"You have heard that it was said, 'An eye for an eye and a tooth for a tooth.' But I say to you, Do not resist the one who is evil. But if anyone slaps you on the right cheek, turn to him the other also. Matt 5:38-39

"You have heard that it was said, 'You shall love your neighbor and hate your enemy.' But I say to you, Love your enemies and pray for those who persecute you, Matt 5:43-44

What Christ is saying is clear. What we have been told in the Old Testament no longer applies. Christ is giving us a new directive. We need to cast out the old and embrace the new; the old is not Christianity. The new is. The old is full of violence; the new is peace. No wonder we have so much violence in the world. We are not practicing Christianity. We are stuck in the old mentality of violence, aggression, taking over someone else's rightful property and confiscating it for ourselves. Imagine Christian clergy blessing soldiers to kill as many as possible of the so-called enemies. Imagine what we did to native peoples. Imagine the horror and the bloodshed inflicted on the Palestinian people. If there was true, pure Christianity, there would have been peace, cooperation and joint ventures in the world long ago instead of the mess we are in.

Christ tells us why He came. He came so we may have life and have it abundantly.

> *The thief comes only to steal and kill and destroy. I came that they may have life and have it abundantly. John 10:10*

Christ did not come to die for our sins. The fact is, He was killed because of our ignorance, blindness, deafness and hard-heartedness. He reminded us of what we can be, but are not—compassionate, forgiving, innocent like children and loving. Most importantly, He told us that we can only love God by loving our fellow humans, our neighbors and even our enemies.

Why 12 Disciples?

Christ had 12 disciples because the number 12 was significant for the ancients for many reasons, mostly because it is the number for completion. The Sun goes through the 12 houses of the Zodiac to complete its cycle. Each house represents a certain quality—6 are positive qualities which we must cultivate and 6 are negative qualities which we must overcome and eradicate. Once we master all 12 qualities, we complete our evolutionary cycle. We become Christlike, masters of our lives and determiners of our fate. Please refer to some of my other books for a detailed description of some of these concepts.

Christ was perfect. We are expected to strive to attain the same status and do all that He did and even more. Here is His admonition to us:

> *You therefore must be perfect, as your heavenly Father is perfect. Matt 5:48*

We cannot attain perfection in a single lifetime. We require many lifetimes to do that and that is why Christ believed in and taught reincarnation.

> *For all the Prophets and the Law prophesied until John, and if you are willing to accept it, he is Elijah who is to come. He who has ears to hear, let him hear. Matt 11:13-15*

In the above quote Christ is clearly stating that Elijah reincarnated as John the Baptist.

The Inner Spiritual Self

Christ must have explained to His disciples what the Kingdom of God within us is. From studying the not-so-obvious meaning of many verses and instances in the life of Christ, I have concluded that the Kingdom of God within us is the ***Inner Spiritual Self***.

We have an outer self, the physical body, and an inner self. The physical body is a mere temple, a house in which the inner self dwells. The physical body is material and upon death it decomposes and reverts back to its earthly components. The physical body is never the same, always changing. It starts as a fertilized ovum, grows, matures and begins to decline and eventually dies. There is nothing in the physical body worth saving.

The inner self has two components: astral and spiritual. The astral self is the **ego.** The ego is where most people function from. The ego is our accumulated habits, attitudes and beliefs. The ego is always in survival mode looking out for its own interests. It is selfish and functions on auto-pilot based on the internal and external forces acting on it. The ego cannot exercise freedom of choice. The ego is where our lower thoughts and emotions reside.

The spiritual self is where our higher thoughts and emotions dwell. It is the **Mustard Seed**, the **Yeast**, the **Treasure**, the **Pearl** and the **Net**. These, however, are dormant in most people. They must be awakened and elevated to a position of royalty so the Kingdom becomes manifest. This is where our true power resides. If we learn to detach, raise our consciousness and function from our spiritual self, then we are truly free, can exercise freedom of choice and make the right decisions. The Inner Spiritual Self is the only aspect of our being that requires saving. We do this by learning to transform our vices into virtues and by spiritualizing the mundane.

The purpose of living, experiencing ups and downs, agonizing and suffering is to wake up to the realization that we must transmute our lower thoughts and feelings into the finer thoughts and emotions of the Inner Spiritual Self. Thus, as we continue to build up our spiritual self, we wake up to who we are and act accordingly. Ultimately, we will have the same experience Jesus had during His baptism when the Holy Spirit descended on Him. Our Inner Spiritual Self is the only permanent aspect of our being. (Please refer to my book: **Know Yourself, Love Yourself and Express Yourself** for a detailed description of these bodies and the purpose of life).

What exactly is the Kingdom of Heaven?

Christ said that the Kingdom of Heaven resides within us.

> *Neither shall they say, Lo here! or, lo there! for, behold, the kingdom of God is within you. Luke 17:21 KJV*

The Kingdom within (the Inner Spiritual Self) is not material. We cannot prove its existence. It is far better to learn how to use its attributes than to discover its existence. To know what these attributes are, we must look at the parables Christ used to describe the Kingdom of Heaven within. He likened the Kingdom within to a seed, yeast, a treasure, a pearl and a net.

Seeds, yeast, treasures, pearls and nets are items of great value. In material terms, they play important roles in our lives. Used as tools, they make a huge difference in the quality of our lives. However, Christ is not teaching us about material wealth. These items are used as allegories alluding to the Inner Spiritual Self.

The Kingdom of Heaven (Inner Spiritual Self) is buried deep within us. It must be discovered, mined, brought to the surface, nurtured and polished for its true value to shine forth.

So, why is the Kingdom of Heaven equated to a seed, yeast, a treasure, a pearl and a net?

Attributes of the Kingdom of Heaven within (the Inner Spiritual Self)

Seed

A seed, unless it is buried in the soil, will not reveal its true nature. A seed is a densely packed potential. A tiny seed can grow into a magnificent tree. Within us lies a dormant spiritual seed. This seed must be awakened and allowed to grow and blossom into a magnificent tree. This tree will bear spiritual fruit—peace, tranquility, contentment and happiness.

A seed is symbolic of **_knowledge_**. Just as a physical seed contains DNA (deoxyribonucleic acid) which "knows" how to blossom into a fully mature plant, our spiritual seed knows how to build the permanent aspect of our being. Unlike DNA, the knowledge within our spiritual seed is not worldly knowledge, but rather spiritual knowledge of how to build our Inner Spiritual Self, expressed as our character and personality.

Knowledge is like a seed that continuously grows. With knowledge we can transform our lives and accomplish the miraculous.

The most important knowledge to have is the ability to make the right decisions at critical junctures in our lives. Knowing that **_we have a choice is of the utmost importance_**. Making the right choices is what sets our lives on the right path. We can choose and by choosing, we can change not only our present status but also our future. Since the wrong choice can lead to disaster, we must know how to choose correctly. In other words, our choices must be based on **_knowledge_**. The right Knowledge has the power to transform lives. This kind of knowledge is founded on three pillars—the heart, the mind and inspiration. These are some of the avenues through which the Inner Spiritual Self expresses itself.

Yeast

Yeast is symbolic of **_inspiration_**. Just as yeast must be mixed in dough and requires an incubation period so does inspiration. While yeast is a fermenting agent, inspiration is a transforming agent. Just as a small amount of yeast can ferment a large quantity of dough, one inspiration can solve complicated problems and alter outcomes dramatically.

Hidden Treasure

Hidden treasure is symbolic of **_intuition_**. Intuition is the gift of knowing without having to think and analyze. It is something we can trust because it wells up from deep within.

While a hidden treasure in the ground must be discovered, dug up, cut and polished before its brilliance can shine forth, intuition comes ready to use. While a hidden treasure once discovered can be converted into immense wealth, intuition can lead to breakthroughs. The ground must be prepared for intuition to appear. What coaxes intuition to burst forth are anticipation, an open mind and a willingness to see, hear and act.

Pearl

A pearl is symbolic of *__life lessons learned through painful experiences__*.

A pearl forms when an irritant enters the shell of a mollusk and calcium carbonate is secreted to counteract the irritation. An irritant can be transformed into something of great value. A pearl can grow from something small and bothersome. We have the power to transmute challenges into opportunities, tragedies into life lessons and irritants into patience and tolerance.

A pearl lives inside a mollusk in the depth of the ocean. It must be retrieved and prepared before its full value is realized.

The "pearl" within us is our life lessons gleaned over many trials and tribulations. It is our irritants that we transform into blessings. It is our pain and suffering that we convert into valuable life lessons that, like a lighthouse, guide our lives. Our challenges are opportunities through which we grow and blossom.

Net

A net is symbolic of *__our magnetic character and personality.__*

A net is critical to a fisherman. With a net, an abundance of fish can be caught. Fishermen who do not realize the critical importance of a net in fishing are misguided novices. With our magnetic character and personality as a net, we can attract into our lives all the abundance we care to have.

* * * * *

Even though we cannot prove the existence of the Kingdom of Heaven within, we cannot deny its attributes. Synchronicities pointing the way for us, knowledge, inspiration, intuition, life lessons from experiences, and character and personality are real and irrefutable.

These are the treasures buried within. They must be discovered and brought to the surface. They must be cultivated, polished and expressed in our daily life as our spiritual qualities. Once developed, they become permanent. They are the only things that do not spoil or that thieves cannot steal. Therefore, the injunction:

> But seek first the kingdom of God and his righteousness, and all these things will be added to you. Matt 6:33

What we need is already within us. We must seek these above all else, for all the treasures of the world are transient; they are not permanent. By discovering and utilizing the attributes of the Kingdom within, we come to know that each of us is a gift of immense value. Within us are transforming agents that can change us from the ordinary to the extraordinary. With these treasures, we get to know ourselves as children of God and each other as brothers and sisters, members of one extended family. We can be transformed into kind, loving and compassionate human beings.

What Salvation Entails

The only aspect of our existence worth saving is our Inner Spiritual Self. The physical body disintegrates, the ego dissipates; only our spiritual component has the capacity to endure. After we die, we can only exist like angels, as spiritual entities.

> But Jesus answered them, "You are wrong, because you know neither the Scriptures nor the power of God. For in the resurrection they neither marry nor are given in marriage, but are like angels in heaven. Matt 22:29-30

Personalizing the Lessons of the Parables of the Kingdom of Heaven

Christ is the New Consciousness, the New Human, "Adam" reborn for the New Age. The New Testament is about The Good News and the good news is that **_we have a choice_**. We can live guided by our egos seeking treasures that spoil and where thieves can break in and steal, or we can choose to live guided by our Inner Spiritual Self where choice and true power reside.

We must care for the physical body because that is where the Inner Spiritual Self resides. We must do what it takes to stay healthy. Gratitude, contentment and living the simple, unencumbered life helps. Not holding grudges, forgiving and loving deeply and intimately go a long way to revitalize and energize us.

The body cannot commit sin. It cannot suffer in the future for it disintegrates upon death and is no more. It is the ego that commits sin via the mind, emotions and uncontrolled urges. Hence, it is the ego that is held accountable. This is why morality is essential to attain spirituality.

> *And he went throughout all Galilee, teaching in their synagogues and proclaiming the gospel of the kingdom and healing every disease and every affliction among the people. Matt 4:23*

When Christ went around healing every disease and every affliction He was mostly working on the hearts and minds of the people. That is what casting off demons means. It is freeing the mind and the emotions from addictive and obsessive behaviors.

It is the Inner Spiritual Self that sets us apart from beasts and distinguishes us from another. By functioning from the ego alone without a well-developed Inner Spiritual Self, we are but beasts in human form. We are "dead" spiritually and do not know it.

> *And Jesus said to him, "Leave the dead to bury their own dead. But as for you, go and proclaim the kingdom of God." Luke 9:60*

> *Jesus answered him, "Truly, truly, I say to you, unless one is born again he cannot see the kingdom of God." John 3:3*

To be born again is for the Inner Spiritual Self to emerge and take center stage. This is the only resurrection there is. The body does not have to be ignored or shunned, rather, its activities need to be spiritualized. We can enjoy life, relationships, love, sex and intimacy. However, we must go beyond the surface and connect our Inner Spiritual Self to the Inner Spiritual Self of others.

The development of our Inner Spiritual Self is paramount. We do this, like Christ taught us, by living a virtuous life, by loving ourselves and others, and by listening to the promptings of The Voice Within. By continuously developing and using the attributes of our Inner Spiritual Self, we become Christlike.

THE SECRET OF CHRISTIANITY

The secret teachings of Christ distill into knowing that we are A LIVING SOUL; we are the Farmer and the Seed, the Yeast and the Dough, the Merchant and the Pearl, the Fisherman and the Net. We are the Sower of the Seeds. We are a vast potential. To actualize this potential, we must work on ourselves. We must transmute our base emotions (tin) into compassion and love (gold). We can spiritualize the mundane by seeing beauty in everything. We can derive joy from everyday activities and we can feel gratitude for all of our blessings. We have an incredible potential that can be actualized as we progressively employ the attributes of the Kingdom of Heaven within—knowledge, inspiration, intuition, life lessons and a magnetic character and personality. With these, every achievement we seek becomes possible.

Why the Parables

- The Kingdom of Heaven within is our Inner Spiritual Self.
- A seed grows and produces fruit and vegetables. Knowledge grows to enrich our lives.
- Yeast ferments dough. Inspiration transforms our lives.
- Intuition is the gift of knowing. It is a treasure beyond value.
- Irritants give rise to pearls. Hardships produce valuable life lessons.
- A magnetic character and personality are nets that attract what we desire.
- Treasures must be dug out and polished. Seeds must be planted before we realize any benefits.
- Used together, the heart, the mind and intuition give us true and lasting **_knowledge_**. The most valuable knowledge is knowing how to make the right choices.
- Knowledge can transform not only our lives, but the entire world as well.
- The best use of the mind is through its higher faculties: visualization, imagination, concentration, contemplation, meditation and prayer.
- The best use of the heart is its higher emotions: love, empathy, compassion and joy.

The Parables from Other Sources

Gospel of Thomas

If those who lead you say, "Look, the kingdom is in heaven," then the birds of heaven will precede you. If they say, "It is in the sea," then the fish will precede you. Rather, the kingdom is within you and outside of you. When you know yourselves, you will be known, and you will know you are children of the living father. But, if you do not know yourselves, you live in poverty and you yourselves are the poverty. (saying #3)

The disciples said to Jesus, "Tell us, what is the kingdom of heaven like?"
He said to them. "It is like a grain of mustard seed, smaller than all seeds. But when it falls on cultivated ground, it puts forth a large branch and provides a shelter for the birds of heaven," (saying #20)

PARABLE OF THE HEART OF MAN

Follow your heart but take your brain with you.
—Alfred Adler

The Parable

And he called the people to him again and said to them, "Hear me, all of you, and understand: There is nothing outside a person that by going into him can defile him, but the things that come out of a person are what defile him." And when he had entered the house and left the people, his disciples asked him about the parable. And he said to them, "Then are you also without understanding? Do you not see that whatever goes into a person from outside cannot defile him, since it enters not his heart but his stomach, and is expelled?" (Thus he declared all foods clean.) And he said, "What comes out of a person is what defiles him. For from within, out of the heart of man, come evil thoughts, sexual immorality, theft, murder, adultery, coveting, wickedness, deceit, sensuality, envy, slander, pride, foolishness. All these evil things come from within, and they defile a person." Mark 7:14-23

The Hidden Meaning

The ancients did not view the heart as we do. The heart was central in their lives. For one thing, the ancients relied much more on intuition than we do. They knew that intuition came from the heart. The heart was the physical and the spiritual center of their being. According to Jack Tresidder's **The Complete Dictionary of Symbols**, the heart is *"the symbolic source of the affections—love, compassion, charity, joy, sorrow—but also of spiritual illumination, truth and intelligence. It was often equated with the Soul."*

According to **The Interpreter's Dictionary of the Bible** *"Of all such organs the heart was the chief; it was the innermost spring of individual life, the ultimate source of all its physical, intellectual, emotional, and volitional energies, and subsequently the part of man through which he normally achieved contact with the divine. In the recesses of the heart dwell the thoughts, plans, attitudes, fears, and hopes which determined the character of the individual."*

Barbara Walker in her **The Women's Encyclopedia of Myths and Secrets** states that the Egyptian *Ab* was the word for **heart and soul**. It was the one that was weighed in the balances of MAAT after death in the Hall of Judgment. From these it is easy to see why Christ says that only what comes out of the heart can defile a person.

What the ancients referred to as the heart is the Inner Self which is both the astral and the spiritual bodies. The inner self controls the heart and the mind. When the astral body (the ego) is in charge, then thoughts and feelings are of a lower nature: fear, jealousy, envy, lust and hatred. When the spiritual self is in charge, then the thoughts and feelings are of a higher nature: love, compassion, empathy and caring. While the ego is the source of what defiles, the spiritual body is the source of what ennobles us.

There seems to be a chemistry between the heart and the mind, a sort of entanglement. They predominantly function together. While the mind provides the ideas, the heart provides the energy to carry out intentions and desires.

When Christ says: *"Do you not see that whatever goes into a person from outside cannot defile him, since it enters not his heart but his stomach, and is expelled?"* it appears that He is talking about food. Any food we consume is clean since it goes to the stomach. This in itself is radical since it goes against all the prohibitions of the Old Testament where we are told what we can eat and what we cannot eat. The above quote continues: *"Thus he declared all foods clean."* This is another instance where Christ is telling us to break free of the Old. We are no longer under the law and governed by numerous commandments.

Then Christ goes on to state that only what comes out of the heart can defile a person: *"For from within, out of the heart of man, come evil thoughts, sexual immorality, theft, murder, adultery, coveting, wickedness, deceit, sensuality, envy, slander, pride, foolishness. All these evil things come from within, and they defile a person."* This makes it clear that He is not talking only about food, but also evil thoughts, intentions and deeds.

Christ is telling us that nothing that we are exposed to can defile us. We can detach from hearing depraved language, watching wicked behaviors or anything that is external and observe them without participating. In other words, we can walk through mud and not get dirty. We can be surrounded by filth and not be contaminated. Only by doing evil ourselves are we held liable.

It is a new era. We can eat pork or anything else we like in moderation. We can sing, dance and do whatever we like. We can live our lives, enjoy ourselves and count our blessings. Christ has set us free. Only the evil that comes from our hearts will be held against us. In the old days, hundreds of commandments enslaved us. Under Christ none of that matters. John the Baptist was among the greatest of the Old. Yet, any true Christian—

spiritual being—is greater than he was.

> *Truly, I say to you, among those born of women there has arisen no one greater than John the Baptist. Yet the one who is least in the kingdom of heaven is greater than he. Matt 11:11*

> "The Law and the Prophets were until John; since then the good news of the kingdom of God is preached, and everyone forces his way into it. Luke 16:16

It is time to put the Old behind us and celebrate the New.

The power of the heart

Reading this parable casually, it appears that Christ is telling us that we can eat whatever we like. There is nothing that we can consume that can defile us. In other words, everything is kosher. But the main force of this parable is to emphasize the power of the heart.

We are accustomed to think that the center of our activities is the mind. For the ancients, it was the heart. While the mind is the center of thinking, the heart is the center of feeling. Thoughts without the accompanying emotions are sterile. What powers thoughts and impels action are the emotions.

Anything that takes place in the heart and mind simultaneously will come to fruition. The most fertile soil is an entangled mind-heart. That is why Christ said the following:

> "You have heard that it was said, 'You shall not commit adultery.' But I say to you that everyone who looks at a woman with lustful intent has already committed adultery with her in his heart." Matt 5:27-28

The Law of Creation

*"Lust is a powerful **desire** coupled with vivid **imagination**. It is based on **knowing** who and what you want. Creation starts in the mind as a vivid impulse, as an idea. If this idea is coupled by a desire for its manifestation, action will follow and the idea will materialize. Any idea accompanied by lust without fear, worry, or doubt, **will** manifest as actual reality. The more positive the expectations, the clearer and more detailed the visualization, the easier it is for that idea to take form and manifest as reality. Therefore, to create a desired experience, we must first fashion it as an idea in the mind and desire it passionately in our hearts. We must see the details of the visualization with great clarity, feel the effects of having achieved the desired end, and with heightened expectation, crave it. This is the law of creation. This is why if we lust for a woman, we have already committed the act. The first phase of creation—ideation—has already taken place. The second phase—manifestation—will inevitably follow.*

This law of creation can be used to acquire anything we desire, or to realize lofty ideals. Looking back, I now see that this is exactly how I immigrated to the United States, found my job, asked for my wife and met her, and wrote this book. This is how I achieve worthwhile goals. I first see the desired outcome clearly in my mind and desire it in my heart. I build the picture in my mind until it is alive and vibrant, and then I release the idea from my mind, trusting that it is done. Once created in the mind, it will manifest physically unless interfered with or sabotaged by doubt, fear and worry.

If creation is as simple as this, it is within the reach of all to partake of its fruit. We are co-creators with God. We create our own destinies, whether we are aware of it or not. It is all in what we choose to "lust" for, expect confidently to attain, and act according to what we desire. Ultimately, what we lust for, becomes our reality."
<u>A Passion for Living</u>, *a path to meaning and joy (Shahan Shammas, available at Amazon.)*

He also told us that *"where your treasure is, there will your heart be also."* In other words, what we treasure and value most should be the noblest of thoughts and feelings because that is where our hearts will also be.

> *Lay not up for yourselves treasures upon earth, where moth and rust doth corrupt, and where thieves break through and steal: But lay up for yourselves treasures in heaven, where neither moth nor rust doth corrupt, and where thieves do not break through nor steal: For where your treasure is, there will your heart be also. Matt 6:19-21*

And if our heart is focused on noble treasures (noble feelings and emotions), then we bring forth that which is good, otherwise we bring forth evil.

> *The good person out of the good treasure of his heart produces good, and the evil person out of his evil treasure produces evil, for out of the abundance of the heart his mouth speaks. Luke 6:45*

Personalizing the Parable

Thus he declared all foods clean.

Superficially, Christ is telling us to eat whatever we like. More importantly, He is breaking away from the Old. If we do not have to abide by the commandments related to eating, we do not have to comply with any commandments of old. What a relief!

Many believe there are 10 commandments in the Old Testament that Moses brought down from the mountain given to him by Yahweh. There are hundreds of commandments governing every aspect of our lives. Reading Leviticus, Numbers and Deuteronomy makes that amply clear.

I came across many of these commandments when I was in the monastery as a young man, studying the Old Testament. I recall these two in particular:

> *The Lord spoke to Moses and Aaron, saying, "Speak to the people of Israel and say to them, When any man has a discharge from his body, his discharge is unclean. And this is the law of his uncleanness for a discharge: whether his body runs with his discharge, or his body is blocked up by his discharge, it is his uncleanness. Every bed on which the one with the discharge lies shall be unclean, and everything on which he sits shall be unclean. And anyone who touches his bed shall wash his clothes and bathe himself in water and be unclean until the evening. And whoever sits on anything on which the one with the discharge has sat shall wash his clothes and bathe himself in water and be unclean until the evening. And whoever touches the body of the one with the discharge shall wash his clothes and bathe himself in water and be unclean until the evening. And if the one with the discharge spits on someone who is clean, then he shall wash his clothes and bathe himself in water and be unclean until the evening. And any saddle on which the one with the discharge rides shall be unclean. And whoever touches anything that was under him shall be unclean until the evening. And whoever carries such things shall wash his clothes and bathe himself in water and be unclean until the evening. Anyone whom the one with the discharge touches without having rinsed his hands in water shall wash his clothes and bathe himself in water and be unclean until the evening. And an earthenware vessel that the one with the discharge touches shall be broken, and every vessel of wood shall be rinsed in water. Lev 15:1-12*
>
> *"When a woman has a discharge, and the discharge in her body is blood, she shall be in her menstrual impurity*

for seven days, and whoever touches her shall be unclean until the evening. And everything on which she lies during her menstrual impurity shall be unclean. Everything also on which she sits shall be unclean. And whoever touches her bed shall wash his clothes and bathe himself in water and be unclean until the evening. And whoever touches anything on which she sits shall wash his clothes and bathe himself in water and be unclean until the evening. Whether it is the bed or anything on which she sits, when he touches it he shall be unclean until the evening. And if any man lies with her and her menstrual impurity comes upon him, he shall be unclean seven days, and every bed on which he lies shall be unclean. Lev 15:19-24

I was young, naïve and impressionable. I believed the Bible to be the Word of God. Reading the above passages, I became utterly distraught. I thought: "How can any young man or young woman be clean if we are plagued by natural bodily discharges?" What if we touch someone or they touch us by accident, then they too will be unclean according to this law.

Thank goodness we do not have to live under the Law anymore. Even though Christ set us free, many "Christians" still choose bondage to the Old rather than breaking free from it. I am hoping this book will have an impact to help people realize that the Old and the Law ended with John the Baptist. The new era of freedom began with Christ and His Good News.

Why the Parable

- Nothing we take in can defile us. We are free to eat whatever we like.
- Only the evil that comes out of the heart can defile us.
- The heart is a very powerful breeding ground. It can breed good or evil.
- What we sow in the heart and mind will germinate and grow.

- The heart is the engine of emotions which power thoughts and impel action.
- The commandments of Old no longer apply to us.
- We can create using our heart, mind and the power of visualization.
- Christ revealed the law of creation by the example of lust.

The Parable from Other Sources

Gospel of matthew

And he called the people to him and said to them, "Hear and understand: it is not what goes into the mouth that defiles a person, but what comes out of the mouth; this defiles a person." Then the disciples came and said to him, "Do you know that the Pharisees were offended when they heard this saying?" He answered, "Every plant that my heavenly Father has not planted will be rooted up. Let them alone; they are blind guides. And if the blind lead the blind, both will fall into a pit." But Peter said to him, "Explain the parable to us." And he said, "Are you also still without understanding? Do you not see that whatever goes into the mouth passes into the stomach and is expelled? But what comes out of the mouth proceeds from the heart, and this defiles a person. For out of the heart come evil thoughts, murder, adultery, sexual immorality, theft, false witness, slander. These are what defile a person. But to eat with unwashed hands does not defile anyone." Matt 15:10-20

Gospel of Thomas

His disciples said to Him, "Is circumcision worthwhile or not?"

He said to them, "If it were worthwhile, their father would beget them already circumcised from their mother. Rather, true circumcision in the spirit has become completely useful. (saying #53)

PARABLE OF THE LOST SHEEP

You have a God who hears you, the power of love behind you, the Holy Spirit within you, and all of heaven ahead of you. If you have the Shepherd, you have grace for every sin, direction for every turn, a candle for every corner and an anchor for every storm. You have everything you need.
—Max Lucado

The Parable

So he told them this parable: "What man of you, having a hundred sheep, if he has lost one of them, does not leave the ninety-nine in the open country, and go after the one that is lost, until he finds it? And when he has found it, he lays it on his shoulders, rejoicing. And when he comes home, he calls together his friends and his neighbors, saying to them, 'Rejoice with me, for I have found my sheep that was lost.' Just so, I tell you, there will be more joy in heaven over one sinner who repents than over ninety-nine righteous persons who need no repentance. Luke 15:3-7

The Hidden Meaning

The emphasis, in this parable, is on the one lost "sheep." We know right away that He is not talking about sheep, but rather people. It is evident that we are the sheep and that every one of us is valued, cared for and expected to be "saved" by discovering his or her shepherd and following it home.

Who the shepherd is, is also clear. It is Christ, for He declared Himself to be The Good Shephard:

> *I am the good shepherd. The good shepherd lays down his life for the sheep. John 10:11*

This shepherd is a good shepherd. He would do anything for His sheep, including laying down His life for them. Imagine that! And why is that? It is because the shepherd is in love with His sheep. This shepherd, however, is not out there in the field. This shepherd is within us, as our Inner Spiritual Self. We are a combination of shepherd and sheep. While the shepherd is the Inner Spiritual Self, the sheep is the ego. For the vast majority, the sheep moves about lost without a shepherd. Christ had pity on us. He incarnated to show us the way to the possible life. This happens when we discover the shepherd within and allow it to lead the way.

> *When he saw the crowds, he had compassion for them, because they were harassed and helpless, like sheep without a shepherd. Matt 9:36*

The shepherd is not ignoring the 99 sheep. They are safe on the mountain or in the valley. The point of the parable is the emphasis on how much we are loved, and that we have a shepherd who will guide us if only we "knock", "ask" and "seek." Then, we will hear the inner voice showing us the way.

Our shepherd often guides us through synchronicities.

This parable clearly demonstrates the break from the Old where the so-called shepherd is a wolf in disguise punishing, judging, and destroying the flock via flood, fire and the sword. While the "shepherd" of the Old is vengeful and vindictive, the one we are told about is so loving and gentle that He will carry us on

His shoulders and give a feast of celebration when we find our way and return home. What a contrast. This is indeed The Good News.

In psalm 23 in the Old Testament, we encounter the shepherd as the Lord.

> The LORD is my shepherd; I shall not want.
> He makes me lie down in green pastures.
>   He leads me beside still waters.
>   He restores my soul.
>   He leads me in paths of righteousness
>   for his name's sake.
>
> Even though I walk through the valley of the shadow of death,
>   I will fear no evil,
> for you are with me;
>   your rod and your staff,
>   they comfort me.
>
> You prepare a table before me
>   in the presence of my enemies;
> you anoint my head with oil;
>   my cup overflows.
> Surely goodness and mercy shall follow me
>   all the days of my life,
> and I shall dwell in the house of the LORD forever.

This is a beautiful psalm but only if we understand who this Lord is. It cannot be an external force to which we abdicate the responsibility for our lives. This Lord is our Inner Spiritual Self, the Christ Consciousness within. When it leads the way, we end up in "green pastures." When the ego leads the way, we have no say in where we will end up.

Another interesting aside to this parable of the lost sheep is that the shepherd is not exclusive to one group of people who consider themselves select or chosen. He is for everyone and is in everyone.

> *And I have other sheep that are not of this fold. I must bring them also, and they will listen to my voice. So there will be one flock, one shepherd. John 10:16*

This parable is analogous to the Parable of the Prodigal Son which we will discuss later.

Why does the shepherd rejoice over the one lost sheep more than over the ninety-nine that never went astray?

One would think it strange to rejoice more over the finding of one lost sheep than the 99 who never went astray. This is the same as when the Prodigal Son returned home and the father rejoiced exceedingly.

Having been lost or leaving the protection of the shepherd is being born into the world. It is being lost in the world through ignorance, temptations and distractions. This is necessary and important. Staying home or with the shepherd is safe and comforting, but we do not have the experience of being on our own. We do not use our own judgment and chart the course of our lives. We do not learn the value of having a home like our Father's or a shepherd like the Christ within. Being lost in the world, we must learn to wake up and find our way home on our own. This will only happen after hardships, pain, suffering and gradual awakening. Eventually we realize the futility of chasing worldly pleasures. They are pleasing, but evanescent. We cannot hold onto them. They are treasures that spoil. Having learned from experience, we head back home.

Wisdom comes from experience. No one can grant us wisdom because no one can experience for us. We must go through the gauntlet and endure. Only difficulties will open our eyes, clear our ears and soften our hearts. Often, the problem with those born in comfort is that they are blind to how the less fortunate live. They have no empathy. It is lack, pain and suffering that soften hearts so we can relate and empathize with the less fortunate. There is no substitute for experience.

Meanwhile, the 99 that stayed safe and secure, lack this essential experience of being in the world alone, insecure and exposed. They do not know fear, insecurity, worry or the feeling of being lost. These are essential for growth and maturity.

Personalizing the Parable

The above parable is about the importance of one single sheep, or an individual who is lost. If we can help one individual find his or her way around in life, then we would have acted like the good shepherd. This parable is telling us that everyone is important, beginning with us. We do not have to opt for grand achievement where we influence the lives of many. That is great when it happens. However, what is more likely is that most of us will have ordinary lives where our sphere of influence is limited. What the parable is telling us is that that is OK. If we can influence the life of just one person and improve the quality of their life, then we should be commended. We do not know how that one change will ripple through time and space and where it will lead. My life was changed dramatically through the kindness and generosity of one individual. The least I can do is repay the favor by touching someone else's life in a positive way.

It is not the numbers and the quantity that matter in the spiritual realm. It is the quality of service rendered. I used to give workshops hoping for large crowds. Often, I would be disappointed. Soon I came to realize that even one benefitting from my lectures is well worth my effort.

It is the same with my books. I write, not because I expect to sell millions of copies, or to be a best seller. I write hoping to influence the life of at least one individual. My mission would then be fulfilled. It is best to do the little we can, rather than expect grandiose achievements. Every change matters. Since we are all connected, each life we touch is well worth our effort. It is like throwing a stone in the water. The rippling effect spreads out on the surface of the water.

Why the Parable

- Everyone is important.
- There is value in going astray if we become wiser as a result.
- We are expected to find our way back by discovering the shepherd within.
- The shepherd within is the Inner Spiritual Self.
- There will be tremendous rejoicing when we return home.
- The shepherd is in love with his sheep.
- If we make a difference in the life of even one individual, then we should be commended.

The Parable from Other Sources

Gospel of Matthew

> "See that you do not despise one of these little ones. For I tell you that in heaven their angels always see the face of my Father who is in heaven. What do you think? If a man has a hundred sheep, and one of them has gone astray, does he not leave the ninety-nine on the mountains and go in search of the one that went astray? And if he finds it,

truly, I say to you, he rejoices over it more than over the ninety-nine that never went astray. So it is not the will of my Father who is in heaven that one of these little ones should perish. Matt 18:10-14

Gospel of Thomas

The kingdom is like a shepherd who had a hundred sheep. One of them, the largest, went astray. The shepherd left the ninety-nine and searched for that one until he found it. After he had labored, he said to the sheep, "I love you more than the ninety-nine." (saying #107)

PARABLE OF THE UNFORGIVING SERVANT

Those who cannot forgive others break the bridge over which they themselves must pass. —Confucius

The Parable

Then Peter came up and said to him, "Lord, how often will my brother sin against me, and I forgive him? As many as seven times?" Jesus said to him, "I do not say to you seven times, but seventy-seven times.

"Therefore the kingdom of heaven may be compared to a king who wished to settle accounts with his servants. When he began to settle, one was brought to him who owed him ten thousand talents. And since he could not pay, his master ordered him to be sold, with his wife and children and all that he had, and payment to be made. So the servant fell on his knees, imploring him, 'Have patience with me, and I will pay you everything.' And out of pity for him, the master of that servant released him and forgave him the debt. But when that same servant went out, he found one of his fellow servants who owed him a hundred denarii, and seizing him, he began to choke him, saying, 'Pay what you owe.' So his fellow servant fell *down and pleaded with him, 'Have patience with me, and I will pay you.' He refused and went and put him in prison until he should pay the debt. When his fellow servants saw what had taken place, they were greatly distressed, and they went and reported to their master all that had taken place. Then his master summoned him and said to him, 'You wicked servant! I forgave you all that debt because you pleaded with me. And should not you have had mercy on your fellow servant, as I had mercy on you?' And in anger his master delivered him to the jailers, until he should pay all his debt. So also my heavenly Father will do to every one of you, if you do not forgive your brother from your heart." Matt 18:23-35*

The Hidden Meaning

This parable is about two things: forgiveness and hypocrisy and both are examples of what Christ is trying to teach us—getting rid of our vices and becoming more virtuous.

Forgiveness

Forgiveness must be very important. That is why Christ says we should forgive *"seventy-seven times."* The number seven implies completion and seventy-seven times means until the forgiveness is fully satisfied. By this Christ does not mean we should keep on forgiving offenders and abusers if they continue their abusing acts. It simply means to forgive completely, wholeheartedly and joyfully.

Forgiveness is a complete release, a letting go of whatever had taken place. It is not words or lip service. Unless it comes from the heart, it does not count. **"Forgive your brother from your heart."** Once more, we see the importance of the heart in matters of the spirit.

Forgiveness benefits the forgiver as much as the forgiven. If we hold onto our grudges and refrain from forgiving, then the resentment will devour us and cause us harm. Forgiving is a release. It frees us. We feel lighter and we can move on with our lives.

Forgiveness is for both mistakes and sins. Mistakes are usually unintentional wrongdoings due to ignorance or carelessness. We are human and liable to make mistakes. We can learn from our mistakes, ask for forgiveness, make amends and move on. Sins are deliberate, intentional, conscious decisions to do what is known to be wrong. There are two "sins" we should seek forgiveness for—sins of commission and sins of omission. The most important person we should forgive is ourselves.

We are not forgiven if we refuse to forgive others. We cannot be hypocrites. Unless we forgive others, we will not be forgiven ourselves.

No one other than the Christ within has the power to forgive. The clergy cannot forgive sins. They have no real spiritual power over us. Besides, our sins are our business and we must deal with them. I remember watching **"The Pillars of Earth"** series where the bishop asks a knight to murder a person. When the knight expresses his fear of going to hell for his act, the bishop forgives him his sin of murder beforehand. Imagine that!

What about confession of sins? The only meaningful confession is to ourselves in the privacy of our conscience. We must review and reflect on our acts of commission and omission regularly, evaluate them and resolve to do better.

Hypocrisy

By telling the parable of the unforgiving servant, Christ demonstrated a deep understanding of human nature. A servant who owes *ten thousand talents* is forgiven his debt. Yet, this same servant refuses to forgive another who owes him *a mere hundred denarii*. Ten thousand talents is a huge amount of money while one hundred denarii is little compared to it. I am not sure if this is due to greed or hypocrisy. The message is clear: We are gifted a tremendous amount. We have freely received the gifts of life and limbs, heart, mind and innumerable blessings of sight, hearing, smell, taste, touch, shelter, food, clothing, beauty all around us, home and family. We are fortunate indeed if we know how to count our blessings. Most of these are free gifts. We are expected, in return, to give back in service.

We are automatically forgiven regardless of what we may have committed or omitted to do. All we have to do is ask sincerely and feel the consequences of our actions in our minds and hearts. We must not only forgive from the heart, but also ask for forgiveness from the heart as well.

We must avoid being hypocrites. I know people who ask for favors when they need them, but they refuse to do the same when asked. It is hypocritical not to treat people the way we would like to be treated. There are people who:

- While suffering injustice complain about the injustice and when they are on the other side, they forget about justice and abuse those they control;
- While imprisoned and tortured, they complain about their treatment and when they have the opportunity, they do not hesitate to imprison and torture others, even worse than they were treated;
- While without a country, these people seek home rule and freedom, yet when they achieve their goal and have a country of their own, they deny the same rights to those under their control.

Hypocrisy is a human disease. It is a vice we must eradicate.

Personalizing the Parable

Living a simple, unencumbered life is a beautiful way to live. Dejunking on an ongoing basis is a wonderful practice. We must dejunk, not only items we no longer need, but more importantly, mental garbage. Forgiving and letting go is a major part of the dejunking process. Whatever anybody did or did not do to us is in the past and is due to ignorance and immaturity. Unless we forgive others, we cannot be forgiven ourselves. Forgiving lightens our burden. It does not imply that we must have relationships with people who wrong us. It simply means letting the bygones be bygone. The past has no power over us unless we allow it. We must look forward and forge ahead. We have a lot we need to accomplish. Why waste our time and energy on the useless when we can invest these in creating the life we choose?

Why the Parable?

- We must forgive before we are forgiven.
- Forgiveness must be from the heart.
- Forgiving helps the one forgiving as much as the one who is forgiven.
- Hypocrisy does not pay.
- We should treat others the way we would like to be treated.
- We have been gifted many blessings. We received freely and freely we should give to others.
- Let us forgive and let go. We will feel lighter and liberated.

PARABLE OF THE LABORERS IN THE VINEYARD

A man who works with his hands is a laborer; a man who works with his hands and his brain is a craftsman; but a man who works with his hands and his brain and his heart is an artist. —Louis Nizer

The Parable

"For the kingdom of heaven is like a landowner who went out early in the morning to hire laborers for his vineyard. After agreeing with the laborers for the usual daily wage, he sent them into his vineyard. When he went out about nine o'clock, he saw others standing idle in the marketplace; and he said to them, 'You also go into the vineyard, and I will pay you whatever is right.' So they went. When he went out again about noon and about three o'clock, he did the same. And about five o'clock he went out and found others standing around; and he said to them, 'Why are you standing here idle all day?' They said to him, 'Because no one has hired us.' He said to them, 'You also go into the vineyard.' When evening came, the owner of the vineyard said to his manager, 'Call the laborers and give them their pay, beginning with the last *and then going to the first.' When those hired about five o'clock came, each of them received the usual daily wage. Now when the first came, they thought they would receive more; but each of them also received the usual daily wage. And when they received it, they grumbled against the landowner, saying, 'These last worked only one hour, and you have made them equal to us who have borne the burden of the day and the scorching heat.' But he replied to one of them, 'Friend, I am doing you no wrong; did you not agree with me for the usual daily wage? Take what belongs to you and go; I choose to give to this last the same as I give to you. Am I not allowed to do what I choose with what belongs to me? Or are you envious because I am generous?' So the last will be first, and the first will be last." Matt 20:1-16*

The Hidden Meaning

A vineyard is a field of transformation where grapes are turned into wine. It is a wedding feast where ordinary water is transformed into delicious wine. It is the world in which we live and where we are expected to change the base into the noble, tin into gold, vice into virtue, challenge into opportunity. It is where we build our character and develop our personality.

The vine is Christ and the vinedresser is the Father. We are branches on this vine.

I Am the True Vine

"I am the true vine, and my Father is the vinedresser. Every branch in me that does not bear fruit he takes away, and every branch that does bear fruit he prunes, that it may bear more fruit. Already you are clean because of the word that I have spoken to you. Abide in me, and I in you. As the branch cannot bear fruit by itself, unless it abides in the vine, neither can you, unless you abide in me. I am

the vine; you are the branches. Whoever abides in me and I in him, he it is that bears much fruit, for apart from me you can do nothing. If anyone does not abide in me he is thrown away like a branch and withers; and the branches are gathered, thrown into the fire, and burned. If you abide in me, and my words abide in you, ask whatever you wish, and it will be done for you. By this my Father is glorified, that you bear much fruit and so prove to be my disciples. As the Father has loved me, so have I loved you. Abide in my love. If you keep my commandments, you will abide in my love, just as I have kept my Father's commandments and abide in his love. These things I have spoken to you, that my joy may be in you, and that your joy may be full. John 15:1-11

We are both physical and spiritual; a body and an inner self. The body is of earth, not of Christ. It will disintegrate and return to earth upon our death. Our inner self, our spiritual aspect is of Christ and if we abide in Christ, that is, if we follow His example of love and service, then we will bear fruit. We cannot bear fruit on our own. We need our connection to our spiritual self, the Christ Consciousness within.

Christ is giving us the formula for an abundant and joyous life. It is to abide in Him. In other words, to push our ego to the background and to do the will of the Higher Self, the spiritual aspect of our inner being.

In the above parable, the vineyard owner does not want laborers to be idle. He brings them to his vineyard to work. He hires some early in the morning, others at 9:00 am, another group at noon, some more at 3:00 pm and finally he hires the last group at 5:00 pm. At 6 pm, he pays his laborers. He pays them all the same daily wage as he promised he would.

This parable is not about fairness or justice. It is

about generosity, envy and most importantly, it is about expectations. The owner is fair because he kept his promise, but because he was generous, envy arose in the hearts of the first shift of laborers. They expected to be paid more than the last group hired who only worked for one hour.

Expectations

Expectations play a major role in our lives. They can make us happy or miserable. If we expect a certain behavior from someone and they behave differently, then we are disappointed. If we go to the dentist expecting the fee to be a certain amount, we become upset if it is much higher. If it is lower, then we are happy. If our boss tells us that we will be getting a financial award we begin speculating what the amount would be. If what we get is lower, we are disappointed. If it is higher, we are elated.

We can learn to manage our expectations so we are never disappointed. We can expect a lot from ourselves. Why not expect far less from others? If we get more than what we expected, then we will be thrilled. For example, if we were to receive a gift, why not expect nothing, or very little? That way we are positively surprised with whatever we get. If it is a fee we must pay, then why not overestimate the cost so we are pleasantly surprised when it is lower. We can still discuss and negotiate afterwards if we need to.

Envy is another vice we need to eliminate. We should practice being thankful for everything that we have already received. There is nothing wrong with striving for more to improve the quality of our lives. If others receive unexpected rewards, why not bless them and celebrate with them? The more we appreciate what we already have, the more blessings will come our way. The more we celebrate others' good fortunes, the healthier and happier we will be.

The Last will be First

Why does Christ say: *"So the last will be first, and the first will be last."*? And why did the last, who worked only for 1 hour, receive the same pay as the first, who worked all day long?

The **first** are the Old, the ones following the Law and the hundreds of commandments. The **last** are the New, the ones following the one commandment—to love and to serve. Those living under the Law have to seek guidance in the commandments as to how to live, what to do and what not to do. Those living in Grace have a light within, a never-failing guide who is the Voice Within, the Christ Consciousness illuminating their way and showing them the path forward. When it's time for an important decision, the promptings of the spiritual self residing within point the way. They listen and act.

While the **first, the Old,** have to labor all day to see results, the **last**, the **New**, can produce great results in no time at all. That is why the first and the last are paid the same. One is Old, using archaic tools and primitive ways to do work, while the New are using advanced spiritual tools such as inspiration, intuition, visualization, imagination and creativity to accelerate and produce quality results in a very short time.

The **first laborers and the Old** are the ones who preceded John the Baptist. The **last laborers and the New** are the followers of Christ. There is no comparison between the two. That is why John the Baptist said the following about Christ:

> *"I baptize you with water for repentance, but he who is coming after me is mightier than I, whose sandals I am not worthy to carry. He will baptize you with the Holy Spirit*

and fire. Matt 3:11

The least in the Kingdom of Heaven (**New**) is greater than he (John the Baptist) (**Old**).

> *Truly, I say to you, among those born of women there has arisen no one greater than John the Baptist. Yet the one who is least in the kingdom of heaven is greater than he. From the days of John the Baptist until now the kingdom of heaven has suffered violence, and the violent take it by force. For all the Prophets and the Law prophesied until John, Matt 11:11-13*

By living the spiritual life one can, in one hour, achieve more than a lifetime of obeying commandments, practicing rituals and going to places of worship. The Old is surface, shallow and mechanical. The New is from the heart, intentional and compassionate.

Personalizing the Parable

We are the laborers in the vineyard. The vineyard is earth. We enter earth at different times. Each laborer has his or her allotted time. Some live for a few years while others live long lives. We come for our own purposes. We need to accomplish the task for which we are in the vineyard. The labor is not easy. The hardships of life will prune us so that we are more "fit" for the Kingdom. Productivity is not a matter of quantity. It is the quality of the products that matter most. Some produce masterpieces in a few short years. Others live long lives leaving nothing memorable behind.

We do not know how long we will live. What is within our power is to use the best methods and tools to achieve quality results in the shortest time. We do this by becoming branches on the vine that is Christ. We discover the treasure buried deep within us. We use our Inner Spiritual Self as a lighthouse to guide our steps. We listen to the Voice Within. We follow its promptings. We do not need hundreds of commandments to know how to live. We need to focus on the vital few and ignore the trivial many. What is enduring is spirituality; the transforming of grapes into wine, tin into gold, vices into virtues, challenges into opportunities for growth.

Why the Parable?

- We are the laborers in the vineyard of life.
- The world is our field. Yet, the most fertile soil is our combined heart and mind. This is where good seeds should be buried.
- Our master is our Inner Spiritual Self.
- Our job is to plant seeds—seeds of confidence, harmony, cooperation, peace and prosperity.
- Idleness is not tolerated. We are expected to work and produce. There are no payments for idle workers.
- It does not matter when we begin our work as long as we do our job earnestly, from the heart.
- In spirituality, it is quality and intent that matter, not quantity and duration.
- Some individuals can do more in 2 hours than others can do all day long.
- We should expect a lot from ourselves and very little from others.
- It is unimportant when we start. What matters is that we are industrious.
- Unlike the laborers in the vineyard, we are already in the world. No one is going to hire us. We are our own bosses.
- We are expected to be proactive and create our own opportunities.

PARABLE OF THE PRODIGAL SON

The difference between mercy and grace? Mercy gave the prodigal son a second chance. Grace gave him a feast.
—Max Lucado

The Parable

And he said, "There was a man who had two sons. And the younger of them said to his father, 'Father, give me the share of property that is coming to me.' And he divided his property between them. Not many days later, the younger son gathered all he had and took a journey into a far country, and there he squandered his property in reckless living. And when he had spent everything, a severe famine arose in that country, and he began to be in need. So he went and hired himself out to one of the citizens of that country, who sent him into his fields to feed pigs. And he was longing to be fed with the pods that the pigs ate, and no one gave him anything.

"But when he came to himself, he said, 'How many of my father's hired servants have more than enough bread, but I perish here with hunger! I will arise and go to my father, and I will say to him, "Father, I have sinned against heaven and before you. I am no longer worthy to be called your son. Treat me as one of your hired servants."' And he arose and came to his father. But while he was still a long *way off, his father saw him and felt compassion, and ran and embraced him and kissed him. And the son said to him, 'Father, I have sinned against heaven and before you. I am no longer worthy to be called your son.' But the father said to his servants, 'Bring quickly the best robe, and put it on him, and put a ring on his hand, and shoes on his feet. And bring the fattened calf and kill it, and let us eat and celebrate. For this my son was dead, and is alive again; he was lost, and is found.' And they began to celebrate.*

"Now his older son was in the field, and as he came and drew near to the house, he heard music and dancing. And he called one of the servants and asked what these things meant. And he said to him, 'Your brother has come, and your father has killed the fattened calf, because he has received him back safe and sound.' But he was angry and refused to go in. His father came out and entreated him, but he answered his father, 'Look, these many years I have served you, and I never disobeyed your command, yet you never gave me a young goat, that I might celebrate with my friends. But when this son of yours came, who has devoured your property with prostitutes, you killed the fattened calf for him!' And he said to him, 'Son, you are always with me, and all that is mine is yours. It was fitting to celebrate and be glad, for this your brother was dead, and is alive; he was lost, and is found.'" Luke 15:11-32

The Hidden Meaning

This parable is similar to the parable of the Lost Sheep. In this case, it is the son who is lost and when he is found by returning home, the father throws a feast in celebration.

The Two Sons

The older son stays with his father and the younger one, takes his inheritance, goes into the world and squanders his wealth.

This son does not think of his home until he hits dirt bottom. He hardly has any food to eat. That is when he remembers his previous glory and decides to return back home and ask for forgiveness.

This younger son is each one of us. We leave the spiritual abode of our Father, come into the world and forget why we are here and what is important. We try out everything, seeking pleasures that do not endure. We keep at it until one day we realize the emptiness of it all. We make an about face, connect with our spiritual kingdom within and focus on what matters most—the development of our spiritual nature.

The older son does not leave his father. He is faithful and responsible. The older son is our Inner Spiritual Self. This son, even though he is with the father, does not realize what that entails. He is unaware of the privileges of being a son. He wants to celebrate with his friends, yet he does not have the courage to do as he pleases. Our Higher Self, the older son, does not need permission to access the bounties of the Father. He merely needs to accept his role as an heir and act accordingly.

We are both of these sons. Our ego is the younger son lost in the world seeking temporary pleasures. Our Spiritual Self is the older son, always with the father. If we live our lives guided by our ego, we will remain lost. Once we discover the Kingdom Within and begin to live a spiritual life, listening to the Voice Within and being guided by our Spiritual Self, then all that our Father has becomes ours. All we have to do is to seek, ask, and knock persistently. The doors to abundance will open.

The Father

Neither the sons nor the father are about gender. The use of the male gender is a reflection of patriarchy in the Middle East. Females are seldom mentioned or highlighted. We see this in the story of Adam and Eve whose children marry without us knowing where the females came from.

The Father is the same one Christ teaches us to address when we pray to God—Our Father who art in heaven. This is another instance where Christ makes the clearcut distinction between two forms of deities. This Father is the antithesis of the deity of the Old. This Father is gentle, loving, non-judgmental, accepting and rejoicing in the return of His Son.

> *"But while he was still a long way off, his father saw him and felt compassion, and ran and embraced him and kissed him."*

Imagine that! Having compassion, not rage and anger. This father does not wait for his son to come to him, he runs towards his son, embraces and kisses him. Christ wants us to be perfectly clear about the deity He is proclaiming to us: loving, never judging, accepting, eager to have us back. He will even throw a feast for us if we decide to return home.

When his older son becomes upset and refuses to come in and join the party, the father goes out and talks to his son. He says: Son, don't you know that all I have is yours? You do not need permission to slaughter a calf to celebrate with your friends. You are at liberty to do as you please. You are the owner as much as I am.

What an amazing father. What compassion, what humility, what tenderness and what love!

Dead or Alive

> *"For this my son was dead, and is alive again; he was lost, and is found."*

This statement is made twice for its significance. Obviously, the younger son was not literally dead, but only spiritually dead and now that he is back, he lives once more. That is why Christ asks us to let the spiritually dead bury their own dead:

> *Another of the disciples said to him, "Lord, let me first go and bury my father." And Jesus said to him, "Follow me,*

and leave the dead to bury their own dead." Matt 8:21-22

We are spiritually "dead" when the ego is in charge of our lives. We "live" once the Inner Spiritual Self takes over and guides our lives.

Personalizing the Parable

We left our Father's house and are on a journey. This is a journey of self-discovery—to know, to love and to express ourselves. On this journey, it is easy to be distracted and lose our way. Difficulties, hardships and challenges will eventually wake us up and we will remember that there is a much better way to live. The sooner we discover the spiritual spark within, the more direct our route home will be.

There is nothing wrong with enjoying all that earth has to offer if we do not abuse or take advantage of anyone else. We can spiritualize every experience through appreciation, thankfulness and full awareness of the significance of the experience.

What is ordinary can be transmuted into the extraordinary. All it takes is awareness and intent. We can spiritualize anything and everything. Our challenge is to go through life seeing beauty in the ugly, squeezing joy from sorrow and extracting love from hate.

All journeys are destined to end and no one knows when our journey will end, so it is best to do what is most important first.

- Cultivate deep and abiding relationships;
- Enjoy the simple pleasures all around us;
- Make the most of our time, skills and abilities;
- Contribute towards the welfare and happiness of others;
- Practice moderation and balance in all that we do;
- Focus on the critical few and seek them first;
    - Relationships

- Continuous education
- Health and
- Productivity
- Cultivate the mind, care for the body and nurture the soul;
- Travel light and burden free;
- Live as if we could die today, with no regrets on our deathbed.

The final destination for our journey is death of the body. Why not enjoy our journey while we can by having fun, savoring life and by being the best we can be—learning, growing and contributing?

Why the Parable?

- To remind us that we are the Prodigal son.
- That we are on a journey and that we have lost our way.
- To be careful about squandering our inheritance—skills, abilities and resources.
- Famines (hardships) can come our way unexpectedly at any time.
- It is best to prepare for famines in lean years, when we have an abundance.
- All that we have is a gift from the Father.
- We have an older brother (Inner Spiritual Self) who is always with our Father.
- Our Father is eagerly waiting for us to return home to him.
- When we do, He will meet us on our way and welcome us with open arms.
- Our Father will put a robe on us, a ring on our finger and shoes on our feet.
- He will slaughter the fatted calf that is saved for special occasions to honor us.

- There will be celebration upon our return home.
- We will not be judged.
- We do not even have to ask for forgiveness. There is nothing to forgive for our Father never holds grudges.
- We are fortunate to have a Father like the one we do.

The real significance of this parable lies in our realization that we are in grace. We will not be judged after we die. Our Father will welcome us home regardless of what we have done or did not do. What a powerful message! What a deviation from all the hell fire messages we have been threatened with. We have nothing to fear. All we need to do is decide that it is time to turn around and head back to our spiritual home. Our first step is to remember who we are—Sons of the Father, Children of God, and last but not least, to know that we are dearly loved.

PARABLE OF THE TENANTS

And yet we are but tenants. Let us assure ourselves of this, and then it will not be so hard to make room for the new administration; for shortly the great Landlord will give us notice that our lease has expired. —Joseph Jefferson

The Parable

And he began to speak to them in parables. "A man planted a vineyard and put a fence around it and dug a pit for the winepress and built a tower, and leased it to tenants and went into another country. When the season came, he sent a servant to the tenants to get from them some of the fruit of the vineyard. And they took him and beat him and sent him away empty-handed. Again he sent to them another servant, and they struck him on the head and treated him shamefully. And he sent another, and him they killed. And so with many others: some they beat, and some they killed. He had still one other, a beloved son. Finally he sent him to them, saying, 'They will respect my son.' But those tenants said to one another, 'This is the heir. Come, let us kill him, and the inheritance will be ours.' And they took him and killed him and threw him out of the vineyard. What will the owner of the vineyard do? He will come and destroy the tenants and give the vineyard to others. Have you not read this Scripture:

> "'The stone that the builders rejected has become the cornerstone;
> this was the Lord's doing, and it is marvelous in our eyes'?"
> Mark 12:1-11

The Hidden Meaning

Why would Christ tell us this parable?

We know all the characters in the parable: the master, the servants, the tenants and the son. This is an important parable because Christ is describing His fate.

The vineyard

The vineyard is our lives, here on Earth. It is where wine is made or where the transformation of grapes into wine is expected to take place. This vineyard is fenced, has a winepress and a tower.

The vineyard, earth, is a place of work where we are expected to turn grapes into wine; or ordinary water into extraordinary wine like Christ demonstrated. Earth is where we form our character and shape our personality. Our job is to transform our challenges into opportunities, our vices into virtues and get to know ourselves by discovering the Inner Spiritual Self and listening to its promptings.

To do this we need a fence to protect and isolate us. We have to be in the world but not of the world. We must learn to deal with dirt and negativity and not be soiled.

The tower

The tower represents our objective to climb ever higher in the evolution of our consciousness. The tower reminds us that we need to be watchful, alert and vigilant. The tower represents our aspirations to do our best and contribute to the welfare of others. In Christianity, the Virgin Mary is known as the "Tower of Ivory" meaning she is pure and an impenetrable fortress.

The work we have to do is not easy. It requires steadfastness, dedication and the willingness to sacrifice. The cost, at times, can be high. The tower is another symbol for cost or the price we have to pay.

Cost

> *For which of you, desiring to build a tower, does not first sit down and count the cost, whether he has enough to complete it? Otherwise, when he has laid a foundation and is not able to finish, all who see it begin to mock him, saying, 'This man began to build and was not able to finish.' Luke 14:28-30*

We must persevere until our work is done, until the building of our tower is complete.

The tenants

The tenants in this parable are the original people chosen to tend the vineyard. They have been entrusted with the vineyard. They were expected to show a profit, a return on the investment for the master, the owner of the vineyard.

The messengers

The messengers are the prophets who were sent to remind the people of old that they need to repay the trust of the vineyard owner by demonstrating that his trust was not misplaced. They needed to live and behave in a prescribed manner. They were not trustworthy. Instead of giving back to the master what was his due, they decided to keep it all for themselves.

Giving back can take many forms. Tithing is one of them, so is setting the Sabbath aside for holy deeds. The idea of giving back is meant for us to dedicate a portion of our time for spirituality. We could pray, meditate, volunteer, reflect on nature, appreciate beauty, listen to uplifting music or read inspiring messages. The spiritual meaning of "giving back" got lost and people assumed that they could not do any work on the Sabbath. Christ demonstrated that this was not so. The Sabbath was for our convenience and not the other way around. We can do noble deeds any time the opportunity presents itself regardless of what day it happened to be.

The owner of the vineyard, God the Father, cares deeply for his children, the tenants. In every age, He sent out his messengers, the prophets, to help remind the people of their duties and obligations. The tenants, having eyes that do not see, and ears that do not hear and hardened hearts, disposed of the messengers. They stoned some, beat others and even killed a few. Finally, the owner decided to send His Son. And what did the tenants do? They killed Him.

The Son

The Son, obviously, is Christ. This parable makes it crystal clear that Christ never came to die for anyone's sins. We killed Him. The parable states that *"they threw him out of the vineyard and killed him."* Taking someone out of the vineyard, is placing the responsibility of the murder on someone else. Instead of killing the son outright, they took him out to Caesar. But Caesar had nothing to do with the murder of an innocent person. Supposedly he washed his hands off the case.

We are the same hypocritical people as the tenants in the parable. Instead of admitting our guilt, we justify the murder of Christ by stating that, "He came to die for our sins and we just carried out His wishes." What a whitewash! Notice that, in the above parable nowhere does the vine owner say that He is sending His son to get killed or to atone for anyone's sins. Original sin and blood sacrifice are human creations and not the nature of a loving and compassionate God. No loving God would ever demand a blood sacrifice, let alone of his own son.

And what does the owner of the vineyard do after the murder of his beloved son? He breaks the lease, fires the old tenants and chooses new tenants instead. And who are these new tenants? They are us with a new lease, under a new set of rules revealed by Christ. Let those who have eyes see and those who have ears hear this new message and abide by its loving terms lest we too are cast out.

The Stone

And what about the stone?

> "'The stone that the builders rejected has become the cornerstone'? Everyone who falls on that stone will be broken to pieces, and when it falls on anyone, it will crush him." Luke 20:17-18

The stone is symbolic of stability, of a rock-solid foundation of faith and self-confidence. The stone is Christ Himself.

> This Jesus is the stone that was rejected by you, the builders, which has become the cornerstone. And there is salvation in no one else, for there is no other name under heaven given among men by which we must be saved." Acts 4:11-12

The "old tenants" rejected this stone, Christ and His message. The "new tenants" must not. His teachings as revealed through the parables must become the cornerstone of our lives. We must live to love and to serve. We must accept everyone and work together in the spirit of peace, harmony and cooperation.

Personalizing the Parable

The days of the vine master sending out messengers or even His own son are over. His Son came and showed us the way. It is up to us now. We have been admonished to seek the Kingdom of

Heaven within. We have been told that Jesus' name is Emmanuel which means God is with us always as our Inner Spiritual Self. We have also been given freedom of choice which we can only exercise if we rise above our ego and function from our Inner Spiritual Self.

We have been given enough prophets, messengers and seers. We have also been given great scientists, physicians, artists, innovators and trendsetters to show us the way. These, too, we shunned, expelled, imprisoned and even killed a few. We are comfortable with our old ways and will not allow anyone to stir the pot.

Amenhotep the Fourth (Akhnaton) was the first in history to expound the worship of the one true God in the form of Aton. He did not last. He was, perhaps, poisoned and dispensed with. We forced Aristotle to decide to drink hemlock. We threw Wilhelm Reich into jail. We killed Martin Luther King. Now the onus is transferred to us individually. Each of us is responsible to do our part to bring more light to our darkened world. If we listen to the Voice Within and act with conscience, we contribute to peace, cooperation and harmony. If we ignore our conscience and remain silent, then nothing will change. We will continue to have wars, strife and atrocities. We have to be the agents of change. It starts with us. We must do our part. Living a spiritual life is not without cost.

If we see an injustice, we have to speak up and do something about it. If we find a cause that needs championing, we should roll up our sleeves and accept the responsibility. It is not going to be easy, but it must be done. Building a tower, raising our consciousness, is costly but necessary. Artists and actors who have spoken up for the rights of the downtrodden in the Middle East have been silenced, threatened with their livelihoods or shunned. The powerful have been abusing their power for far too long. Fortunately, temporal power is temporary. Real power is that of character and inner strength. Spirituality is the new way. It is our only hope for a bright and peaceful future.

Why the Parable?

- The tenants of old ignored the messengers; we should not.
- The tenants of old were self-absorbed; we should not do the same.
- We live in a vineyard. Transforming grapes into wine should be our job description. Transforming our challenges into opportunities, our vices into virtues is how we do it.
- Building our Inner Spiritual Self is not without cost; we must be willing to pay the price.
- Our master is patient, but there is a limit to the master's patience. A good-faith return on investment must be demonstrated.
- We are foolish to believe that by killing the Son, we get His inheritance.
- The only way to inherit the Father's abundance is to become one of His children.
- Christ is the stone and His teachings are the foundation on which we should base our lives.

The Parable from Other Sources

Gospel of Matthew

"Hear another parable. There was a master of a house who planted a vineyard and put a fence around it and dug a winepress in it and built a tower and leased it to tenants, and went into another country. When the season for fruit drew near, he sent his servants to the tenants to get his fruit. And the tenants took his servants and beat one, killed another, and stoned another. Again he sent other servants, more than the first. And they did the same to

them. Finally he sent his son to them, saying, 'They will respect my son.' But when the tenants saw the son, they said to themselves, 'This is the heir. Come, let us kill him and have his inheritance.' And they took him and threw him out of the vineyard and killed him. When therefore the owner of the vineyard comes, what will he do to those tenants?" They said to him, "He will put those wretches to a miserable death and let out the vineyard to other tenants who will give him the fruits in their seasons." Matt 21: 33-41

Gospel of Luke

And he began to tell the people this parable: "A man planted a vineyard and let it out to tenants and went into another country for a long while. When the time came, he sent a servant to the tenants, so that they would give him some of the fruit of the vineyard. But the tenants beat him and sent him away empty-handed. And he sent another servant. But they also beat and treated him shamefully, and sent him away empty-handed. And he sent yet a third. This one also they wounded and cast out. Then the owner of the vineyard said, 'What shall I do? I will send my beloved son; perhaps they will respect him.' But when the tenants saw him, they said to themselves, 'This is the heir. Let us kill him, so that the inheritance may be ours.' And they threw him out of the vineyard and killed him. What then will the owner of the vineyard do to them? He will come and destroy those tenants and give the vineyard to others." When they heard this, they said, "Surely not!" But he looked directly at them and said, "What then is this that is written:

"'The stone that the builders rejected has become the cornerstone'?

Everyone who falls on that stone will be broken to pieces, and when it falls on anyone, it will crush him." Luke 20:9-18

Gospel of Thomas

A good man had a vineyard. He leased it to some farmers so that they would cultivate it and he would receive the fruit from them. He sent his servant so that the tenants would give him the fruit of the vineyard. They seized his servant, beat him and almost killed him. The servant returned and told his master. The master said, "perhaps they did not recognize him." He sent another servant. The tenants beat him also. Then the master sent his son. He said, "Perhaps they will respect my son." The tenants, knowing he was the heir to the vineyard, seized the son and killed him. Whoever has ears let him hear. (saying #65)

PARABLE OF THE WEDDING FEAST

Uninvited guests are often most welcome when they leave.
 —Aesop

The Parable

And again Jesus spoke to them in parables, saying, "The kingdom of heaven may be compared to a king who gave a wedding feast for his son, and sent his servants to call those who were invited to the wedding feast, but they would not come. Again he sent other servants, saying, 'Tell those who are invited, "See, I have prepared my dinner, my oxen and my fat calves have been slaughtered, and everything is ready. Come to the wedding feast."' But they paid no attention and went off, one to his farm, another to his business, while the rest seized his servants, treated them shamefully, and killed them. The king was angry, and he sent his troops and destroyed those murderers and burned their city. Then he said to his servants, 'The wedding feast is ready, but those invited were not worthy. Go therefore to the main roads and invite to the wedding feast as many as you find.' And those servants went out into the roads and gathered all whom they found, both bad and good. So the wedding hall was filled with guests.

"But when the king came in to look at the guests, he saw

there a man who had no wedding garment. And he said to him, 'Friend, how did you get in here without a wedding garment?' And he was speechless. Then the king said to the attendants, 'Bind him hand and foot and cast him into the outer darkness. In that place there will be weeping and gnashing of teeth.' For many are called, but few are chosen." Matt 22:1-14

The Hidden Meaning

The Setting

The setting is similar to many parables where a wedding feast is involved.

God is the host, Christ is the groom, *"a king who gave a wedding feast for his son."*

There are two types of guests, those who are invited and those who are not. We are the guests. Initially, only a few received invitations. With the coming of Christ, all have an open invitation to join in the festivities. All we have to do is accept the invitation, open our hearts and minds and dedicate a small portion of our time pursuing spirituality. This would be our wedding gift.

Weddings are the celebration of the union of the bride and the groom. In our case, the union of the outer self, the ego with the Inner Spiritual Self. The bride and the groom are expected to be pure. Nuns are symbolic of purity. Their marriage is to Christ; thus, they remain celibate. The required purity, however, is not of the body. It is spiritual purity, that of the mind and the heart. Physical purity is external. Spiritual purity is internal. Physical purity does not necessitate abstinence from the joy of living. We can be intimate, have sex and get physical and remain pure if we carry out our activities in love, with caring and mutual appreciation. What has to be pure is our intent. If we are driven by our passions and the ego, then we can never be pure. If our driver is the Inner Spiritual Self, then we are always pure. This is where the idea of virginity came from—virginity of the heart and spirit. The body does not have a volition of its own. Mind and intent are the driving forces. They are the key players and only they can be pure or impure.

Who are the original guests?

The invited guests are the people of the Covenant, the people under the Law, the ones who consider themselves "the chosen." Yet, they refused the invitation making excuses as to why they cannot attend the celebration. The true reason they did not want to attend the wedding feast is because it did not fit their expectations. They were waiting for a temporal king who would lead them into war and to victory over the Romans, as all of their other ancient leaders did before. But Christ is not such a leader. He is a spiritual king and His kingdom is not of earth. Instead of accepting the invitation and joining the feast, the original invitees turned down the invitation. They did not want to change their ways. Christ's teaching was such a radical departure from the expected, that very few accepted and followed Him. The original guests did not want to feast on the new teachings—love, service and empathy. They preferred war and carnage. So, they were excluded, more appropriately, they excluded themselves.

Who are the new guests?

The new guests included anyone and everyone; street people, common ordinary people, good and bad people, well-off people and beggars comprising all nationalities and ethnic groups. All they have to do to get to the feast was to accept "the good news" and to "dress" accordingly.

> "But when the king came in to look at the guests, he saw there a man who had no wedding garment. And he said to him, 'Friend, how did you get in here without a wedding garment?' And he was speechless. Then the king said to

the attendants, 'Bind him hand and foot and cast him into the outer darkness. In that place there will be weeping and gnashing of teeth.' For many are called, but few are chosen."

"Dressing" for the wedding is having the right attitude—open eyes, clear ears and an empathetic heart willing to change, to forgive, to love and to serve.

Personalizing the Parable

We can live life in celebration as if we are at a wedding feast where everything is set up for our enjoyment. These are the free gifts of life—natural beauty, intimacy and friendship. There is a lot we can enjoy, but first we have to have eyes that see, ears that hear and hearts that feel.

We can choose to see beauty where there is none.
We can opt to hear music and melodies where there is discord.
We can touch, and in touching, we can feel warmth, tenderness and love.
We can taste to savor.
We can be mental Alchemists and transform foul odors into aromas and fragrances.
We can live a wondrous life where we are constantly transforming the ordinary into the extraordinary.
We can feel joy and experience love anytime we choose. It is a choice and we must consider it seriously.

Why the Parable?

- We are invited to a wedding where a feast is prepared for us.
- All we have to do is to stop making excuses and accept the invitation.
- Since the original invitees refused to attend, the doors for this wedding feast opened up to all without

exception.
- To be a worthy guest, we must dress accordingly with humble hearts and a willingness to love and to serve. This is why *"many are called, but few are chosen."*
- Whatever we do for others has to be gratuitous without ever expecting anything in return.
- *"None of those men who were invited shall taste my banquet."* To taste of the banquet is to experience a life of peace, tranquility, love and joy.
- The banquet is the Kingdom of Heaven manifesting on Earth. We, the invitees, make it happen.

The Parable from Other Sources

Gospel of Luke

He said also to the man who had invited him, "When you give a dinner or a banquet, do not invite your friends or your brothers or your relatives or rich neighbors, lest they also invite you in return and you be repaid. But when you give a feast, invite the poor, the crippled, the lame, the blind, and you will be blessed, because they cannot repay you. For you will be repaid at the resurrection of the just."

When one of those who reclined at table with him heard these things, he said to him, "Blessed is everyone who will eat bread in the kingdom of God!" But he said to him, "A man once gave a great banquet and invited many. And at the time for the banquet he sent his servant to say to those who had been invited, 'Come, for everything is now ready.' But they all alike began to make excuses. The first said to him, 'I have bought a field, and I must go out and see it. Please have me excused.' And another said, 'I have bought five yoke of oxen, and I go to examine them. Please have me excused.' And another said, 'I have married a

wife, and therefore I cannot come.' So the servant came and reported these things to his master. Then the master of the house became angry and said to his servant, 'Go out quickly to the streets and lanes of the city, and bring in the poor and crippled and blind and lame.' And the servant said, 'Sir, what you commanded has been done, and still there is room.' And the master said to the servant, 'Go out to the highways and hedges and compel people to come in, that my house may be filled. For I tell you, none of those men who were invited shall taste my banquet.'"
Luke 14:12-24

Gospel of Thomas

A man had the habit of receiving visitors. When he had prepared a banquet he sent his servant to invite the guests. The servant went to the first and said to him, "My master invites you." The man replied, "Money is owed me by some merchants. They will come to me this evening; I must go and give them orders. I beg to be excused from the dinner."

The servant went to another and said to him, "My master has invited you." The second man said to him, "I have just bought a house and am needed for a day. I have no time."

The servant went to another and said to him, "My master invites you." That man said. "My friend is about to be married and I have to prepare a wedding feast; I will not be able to come, I beg to be excused from the dinner."

The servant went to another and said to him, "My master invites you." He said to the servant, "I have bought a village and am on my way to collect the rent. I will not be able to come, I beg to be excused from the dinner."

The servant returned and said to the master, "Those you invited asked to be excused from the dinner." The master *said to the servant, "Go out into the streets and bring in those whom you find so that they may dine."*

Buyers and merchant will not enter the places of my father. (saying #64)

PARABLE OF THE BARREN FIG TREE

No greater thing is created suddenly, any more than a bunch of grapes or a fig. If you tell me that you desire a fig, I answer you that there must be time. Let it first blossom, then bear fruit, then ripen. —Epictetus

The Parables

And he told this parable: "A man had a fig tree planted in his vineyard, and he came seeking fruit on it and found none. And he said to the vinedresser, 'Look, for three years now I have come seeking fruit on this fig tree, and I find none. Cut it down. Why should it use up the ground?' And he answered him, 'Sir, let it alone this year also, until I dig around it and put on manure. Then if it should bear fruit next year, well and good; but if not, you can cut it down.'"
Luke 13: 6-9

The Lesson of the Fig Tree

And he told them a parable: "Look at the fig tree, and all the trees. As soon as they come out in leaf, you see for yourselves and know that the summer is already near. So also, when you see these things taking place, you know that the kingdom of God is near. Truly, I say to you, this

generation will not pass away until all has taken place. Heaven and earth will pass away, but my words will not pass away. Luke 21:29-33

The Hidden Meaning

The barren fig tree

When Christ looked at a fig tree, He expected to find fruit on that tree. The fig tree is a symbol of abundance and fecundity. He, not only expected fruit, but expected it abundantly. Since the tree is symbolic of the people who have been "prepared and groomed to produce fruit," He expected results in and out of season. While there are seasons for trees to produce fruit, people are expected to be productive at all times. That is why in the parable of the Laborers in the Vineyard, idle workers are not appreciated:

> *and he said to them, 'Why are you standing here idle all day?' They said to him, 'Because no one has hired us.' He said to them, 'You also go into the vineyard.'*

What type of fruit are we expected to produce? The fruit stemming from the Christ Consciousness: love, acceptance, forgiveness, compassion, humility, faith and service. Producing fruit should be as natural as a fig tree produces figs—instinctively, naturally and without labor or effort. We do not have to do much. Being a lighthouse radiating our Christ Consciousness as the aroma of our being and as our natural state is good enough. It will infuse the atmosphere and change the environment.

> *You will recognize them by their fruits. Are grapes gathered from thornbushes, or figs from thistles? So, every healthy tree bears good fruit, but the diseased tree bears bad fruit. A healthy tree cannot bear bad fruit, nor can a diseased tree bear good fruit. Every tree that does not bear good fruit is cut down and thrown into the fire. Thus you will recognize them by their fruits.* Matt 7:16-20

The vinedresser addresses Christ saying: *'Sir, let it alone this year also, until I dig around it and put on manure. Then if it should bear fruit next year, well and good; but if not, you can cut it down.'* In other words, let us give these people another opportunity to prove themselves. We will expose them to your parables and to your sermons and if they change and produce acceptable results, we will be satisfied. Otherwise, we have no option but to move on and look for other "fig trees"—other people who are willing to see, hear, accept and bear fruit abundantly.

The end time is near

Many believe that Christ was alluding to the end days when He referred to the budding fig tree as the sign to look for. Then He elaborated:

> *Truly, I say to you, this generation will not pass away until all these things take place.*

What He is talking about is the coming of the Kingdom of Heaven. Summer and the Kingdom of God are near. Summer is the harvest time. The Kingdom of God is within us as our Inner Spiritual Self. In other words, before this generation passes away, there will be many who would have discovered the Kingdom of God within, developed their Inner Spiritual Self and would have borne fruit. Obviously, this is true since all those He taught secretly (mostly His disciples) not only received Christ's message, but understood it as well. The disciples dedicated their remaining days to spreading the Gospel of the Good News.

Many believe that Christ, like John the Baptist and many others, was apocalyptic. For these people, the references to the end of days was about the physical end of life on earth as we know it. In other words, they believed in a literal coming of the Kingdom of Heaven where God and his angels will descend from heaven and wage war against Satan and his devils. Obviously, God would win. The dead will be resurrected and judgment will take place. Those hearing Christ say that His Kingdom was not from this world, believed that in the new Kingdom, Jesus will be crowned king and rule with His disciples over the 12 tribes of Israel. It is easy to infer this from the following statements:

> *Jesus said to them, "Truly, I say to you, in the new world, when the Son of Man will sit on his glorious throne, you who have followed me will also sit on twelve thrones, judging the twelve tribes of Israel. Matt 19:28*

> *"You are those who have stayed with me in my trials, and I assign to you, as my Father assigned to me, a kingdom, that you may eat and drink at my table in my kingdom and sit on thrones judging the twelve tribes of Israel. Luke 22:28-30*

The literal interpretation of these statements creates an insurmountable obstacle. Christ is addressing His 12 disciples as future rulers over 12 kingdoms and as judges over the 12 tribes of Israel. We know, as documented in The Last Supper, that Christ knew Judas Iscariot will betray Him. This disciple will hang himself and will not be available to rule. Historically, there were never 12 tribes of Israel. They were never lost because they never existed. If Christ and His disciples will rule over the 12 tribes of Israel, what about all the other people on the planet? Who will rule and judge them? Are the Jews the only people on the planet that are of any consequence?

From the following statement by Christ, it is evident that in the coming Kingdom of Heaven, people will not be in their physical bodies. They will be in their spiritual bodies.

> *But Jesus answered them, "You are wrong, because you know neither the Scriptures nor the power of God. For*

> *in the resurrection they neither marry nor are given in marriage, but are like angels in heaven. Matt 22:29-30*

If after the resurrection, we are like angels, then we cannot be physical. Angels do not have physical, material bodies. Christ is not concerned with the material, only with the spiritual.

What Christ stated publicly cannot be the essence of His teachings—His parables and private teachings to His disciples are. What Christ said publicly was for His audience and in accordance with what this audience understood and expected to hear. Additionally, these statements are not reliable since they were tampered with. The original copies of the gospels are lost. What we have are copies of copies that have been copied over and over from one generation to the next and in several countries over hundreds of years. They have been mistranslated, altered, added to and subtracted from. Those making the copies were not official scribes, just ordinary people like you and me. In the Syriac Orthodox church where I grew up, the Bible we used was a hand written copy in Syriac (Aramaic). Keep in mind that the printing press was not invented until 1440 A.D.

We do not know what Christ taught His disciples in secret. We do know quite a lot about what He secretly encoded in the parables. He makes it clear that His messages were rejected by the ones He taught. His life demonstrates that He is not the expected Messiah. He is a prince of peace, not of war, a gentle soul, not a conqueror. He wants to do away with the Old and usher in the New. The Old served its purpose. It is time for a new age, an age where love reigns supreme and where compassion, tolerance, acceptance and service are the norm. Since the Chosen refused Him, the door opened wide for a new diverse group of people from all over the land to come in and participate in the feast. From the parables, we come to realize that Christ's Kingdom of

Heaven is within and that it can be accessed by anyone with the proper intention. How else can this Kingdom of Heaven be compared to a mustard seed, a leaven, a pearl, a treasure and a net? We must dig for this buried treasure, discover it, unearth it, polish it and make it the centerpiece of our lives.

Personalizing the Parable

The message of the parable of the fig tree is clear. It is about what is expected of us. We are expected to be productive. It is the reason we are on earth in the first place. The parable makes it clear that being barren or non-productive is unacceptable. Idleness will not be tolerated. Time is of the essence, not because there is an end to our days, but because of the preciousness of our being here. Earth provides us with the opportunities we need to wake up, discover who we are, why we are here and what we need to do with our lives. Earth is not only a vineyard loaded with hanging grapes, it is an orchard and a garden. The diversity of earth is mind boggling. We can experience everything and anything imaginable on this beautiful and astonishing planet. It is indeed a privilege to be here, alive at this time.

Why the Parable?

- Fruit trees are expected to produce fruit. People are expected to be productive.
- We have been given Christ's teachings as fertilizer that we must incorporate into our lives to be spiritually productive.
- The end days are for the old way of life. Those days are numbered. The Old remains with us because most have not woken up to what resides within them—The Christ Consciousness as the Kingdom of God within.

The Parable from Other Sources

Matthew (The Budding Fig Tree)

"From the fig tree learn its lesson: as soon as its branch becomes tender and puts out its leaves, you know that summer is near. So also, when you see all these things, you know that he is near, at the very gates. Truly, I say to you, this generation will not pass away until all these things take place. Heaven and earth will pass away, but my words will not pass away. Matt 24:32-35

PARABLE OF THE FAITHFUL VS. THE WICKED SERVANT

Trust is the easiest thing in the world to lose, and the hardest thing in the world to get back. —R. M. Williams

The Parables

The parable according to Matthew

"Who then is the faithful and wise servant, whom his master has set over his household, to give them their food at the proper time? Blessed is that servant whom his master will find so doing when he comes. Truly, I say to you, he will set him over all his possessions. But if that wicked servant says to himself, 'My master is delayed,' and begins to beat his fellow servants and eats and drinks with drunkards, the master of that servant will come on a day when he does not expect him and at an hour he does not know and will cut him in pieces and put him with the hypocrites. In that place there will be weeping and gnashing of teeth. Matt 24:45-51

The parable according to Mark

It is like a man going on a journey, when he leaves home and puts his servants in charge, each with his work, and *commands the doorkeeper to stay awake. Therefore stay awake—for you do not know when the master of the house will come, in the evening, or at midnight, or when the rooster crows, or in the morning— lest he come suddenly and find you asleep. And what I say to you I say to all: Stay awake." Mark 13:34-37*

The Hidden Meaning

The world is a diversity of people. Some are good, others are bad or even evil while the majority are somewhere in between. We cannot deny that evil people exist. These are the ones who take advantage of others or situations to further their own good at the expense of others. While good people know that their good fortune is a responsibility, evil people abuse their position and take advantage of their good fortune.

We must never forget that whatever we have, we hold in trust. Our status, title and possessions are temporary. Our stay in the body has an expiration date. We are all servants of one kind or another. None of us is a master. Driven by our ego, we assume we are important, powerful, and capable of many wonderful things. All of our abilities, however, are gifts. We could lose them at any time and when we do, we realize that we never really had them to begin with. This happens when we are very sick or disabled. It is then that we realize that all we have are gifts.

If we are in a position of power, we should assume that we have been entrusted with that power to serve. It is not for our glorification. The secret of happiness is not by taking from others or by ruling over them. It is by serving, by giving back and by ensuring the happiness of others.

We reap in accordance with what we sow. If we sow grape seeds, we will end up with a vineyard. If we allow thorns to grow in our soil, then our life will be miserable.

Who are the faithful servants?

These are the ones who understand that their power has been delegated by their master. It is not a power to rule over their fellow employees. It is an opportunity to demonstrate management skills, to make a positive contribution and to improve the status quo. They know that their selection to be in charge is not a license to rule. These faithful servants are loyal, humble and fair. They always do the best they can. They set an example of what service should be. They are first in line to do their part. They give more than what is expected of them. They are eager to contribute and to empower. And when the master returns, because they have been faithful with the little, more and better responsibilities will be given to them.

Who are the wicked servants?

These are the ones who take advantage of their position to enrich themselves. They care less about anyone else. Their attitude is: "It is us against the world." They abuse their position of power. They unjustly impose their will on the less fortunate. They side with their friends and allies, right or wrong. They are proud, arrogant and haughty. As long as they are in power, they believe they are invincible. Power, however, is fickle. What has been given can be taken away. What is up today can and will come down tomorrow. It is only a matter of time before their fortunes change.

Power is responsibility. It is a temporary trust and no one knows how long it will last. The wicked servants, while they have their power, are on top of the world. When that power is gone, they will fall into the bottomless pit from which there is no escape. *"In that place there will be weeping and gnashing of teeth."* In other words, this is where one reflects on the consequences of one's actions. This is where the "weighing of the soul against the feather of truth" happens. It is best to review our actions while we live rather than wait until after we die when there is little we can do other than feel sorrow, regret and self-pity.

Staying awake

No one knows when our end will come. Therefore, staying awake is imperative. We are urged to not fall asleep, to stay awake, to keep our spiritual eyes open, our spiritual ears clear and our hearts beating with life, love and compassion.

Staying awake is always being ready for what may come. We have been preparing all of our lives for this current moment. We are ready to handle any situation that comes our way. Our bodies are fit, our minds are sharp, our emotions are mature. Our intuition is awakened and our antennas are set to receive the promptings of the Voice Within and act upon them.

Personalizing the Parable

How do we become faithful servants?

We become faithful servants by being diligent, prepared and ready to act when the opportunity comes our way. We are eager to praise, to serve and to empower. By acting nobly, we become worthy of what we have been entrusted with.

We know that our position of power is a responsibility and a trust and we act accordingly. By making a difference in the life of even one individual, preferably anonymously, is enough to put us in the good servant column.

How do we become wicked servants?

It is easy and tempting to be a wicked servant. Even being indifferent places us in that category. While it is natural to be wicked, it takes intention, awareness and effort to be the faithful servant.

Why the Parable?

- Life is an opportunity to prove ourselves.
- We have a choice of being faithful or wicked servants.

- We must stay awake and be diligent.
- We must give our best in service.
- Remaining humble is praiseworthy.
- We will always have a master toward whom we will be held accountable.
- Our master resides within us as our conscience.

PARABLE OF THE TEN VIRGINS

By failing to prepare, you are preparing to fail.
—Benjamin Franklin

The Parable

"Then the kingdom of heaven will be like ten virgins who took their lamps and went to meet the bridegroom. Five of them were foolish, and five were wise. For when the foolish took their lamps, they took no oil with them, but the wise took flasks of oil with their lamps. As the bridegroom was delayed, they all became drowsy and slept. But at midnight there was a cry, 'Here is the bridegroom! Come out to meet him.' Then all those virgins rose and trimmed their lamps. And the foolish said to the wise, 'Give us some of your oil, for our lamps are going out.' But the wise answered, saying, 'Since there will not be enough for us and for you, go rather to the dealers and buy for yourselves.' And while they were going to buy, the bridegroom came, and those who were ready went in with him to the marriage feast, and the door was shut. Afterward the other virgins came also, saying, 'Lord, lord, open to us.' But he answered, 'Truly, I say to you, I do not know you.' Watch therefore, for you know neither the day nor the hour. Matt 25: 1-13

The Hidden Meaning

Kingdom of Heaven

The Kingdom of Heaven is likened to 10 virgins going to a wedding feast.
To be a virgin is to be pure. If the wedding feast is the Kingdom of Heaven, then no one but those with pure intention, heart and mind may enter.

Like the Vestal Virgins of old, these young ladies have dedicated their lives to serve a particular deity. Vestal Virgins served the goddess Vesta. They were spiritually pure, but not necessarily physically virginal. According to Barbara Walker, author of **The Women's Encyclopedia of Myths and Secrets**, *"the Vestals were never altogether virginal in the physical sense. Their marriage to the phallic deity Palladium was physically consummated in Vesta's temple, under conditions of great secrecy. The ceremony was performed by a priest called the Pontifex Maximus, 'great maker of the pons,' which meant a bridge, a path or a way."* The focus then is not on physical purity, but rather purity of intention, heart and mind. Anyone who has a pure heart is a virgin regardless of carnal experience as long as these experiences are based on mutual love, affection and honoring.

Number 10

Ten is the perfect number, symbolizing the cosmos and all manifestation. Ten contains all the digits from zero to nine. Hence, it is what contains all. In this parable, 10 represents all of humanity.
(Please refer to Appendix B for an explanation of ***The Esoteric Significance of Numbers***).

Number 5

Five is the number for the human being with outstretched arms and legs and with the head making the figure of the pentagram. Humanity is divided into wise and foolish individuals. The wise ones are guided by their Inner Spiritual Self. They employ heart, mind and intuition in their daily affairs. The foolish ones are guided by their passions and the ego. They live for the moment seeking pleasure and immediate gratification.

Lamp

Source of light, the Inner Self, the Christ Consciousness within. The virgins with the lamps are the pure tending the eternal flame symbolizing the zeal of the heart.

Flasks of oil

Oil is what keeps the light within burning. Oil represents faith, trust, confidence, zeal, inner strength and steadfastness. These are the extra reserves we need to have in case of an emergency.

Bridegroom

Opportunity.

Drowsiness and Sleep

Getting tired which happens to all of us can lead to drowsiness and sleep. It results from boredom, inattentiveness and lack of vigilance.

Midnight

Midnight is when the unexpected happens. This is when it is darkest; the unforeseen lurks in darkness.

A cry: "Here is the bridegroom. Come out and meet

Him."

Surprise. When opportunity knocks, are we ready to open the door and take advantage of the situation?

The foolish 5

These are the unprepared. The foolish ones do not carry enough oil in reserve. They are the ones who squander their time, skills and abilities. They are unprepared for emergencies.

The wise 5

These are the faithful, diligent and wise ones. These individuals use their time, skills and abilities wisely. They are always ready and prepared for the unexpected.

While they (the foolish) were gone

While the foolish were distracted, focused on the unimportant and were inattentive, the unexpected happened. We must be ready and prepared before an unexpected emergency, not get ready during the emergency.

Those who were ready went into the marriage feast

When we are ready, we can take advantage of any opportunity that presents itself. We must live life as if we are at a marriage feast, enjoying and celebrating every moment. The marriage is that of the ego, the outer self, with the Inner Spiritual Self. The ego is the bride (the material) while the Inner Spiritual Self is the bridegroom. Unless the ego is pure (virginal), it cannot unite with the spiritual. Marriage is between two equals.

Watch out. We do not know the day or the hour

Life is unpredictable. We must be vigilant and ready at all times. Our antennas should be tuned to listen to the Voice Within. When opportunity knocks, we are ready to open the door and act. When the Voice Within speaks, we never hesitate to respond.

Personalizing the Parable

Christ has given us the formula for success and happiness in life. Material success is important to provide for our needs and necessities. Spiritual success is permanent success. It becomes an aspect of our character and personality.

We must be like the five wise virgins living preventive lives. We must be ready for any eventuality. One day the big wigs at work convened an off-site conference. Since I was acting for my boss, I had the opportunity to attend on her behalf. We broke out into small groups to discuss various topics. One of the managers in my group, disliked me outright for no apparent reason. At the end of our discussions, one of us was to be tasked with presenting our findings to the top-level managers the next morning. I was acting as an observer since I was not a manager. Yet, to humiliate me, this manager who disliked me volunteered me with the task of presenting our findings to management the next morning.

Initially, I panicked. I had not taken notes because I never expected to do anything but observe. I realized that this was a major challenge and that I had to find a way to convert this into an opportunity. I went into the woods, isolated myself and meditated on my situation. Soon ideas began to flood my mind. I wrote them down. After a while, I was ready, cool and calm.

The next morning, while shaking, I stepped forward and gave my presentation. I was in my zone and as if a higher power overtook me, the presentation flowed impeccably. The managers were stunned and so was my next level manager. He approached me, congratulated me and told me that he never knew that someone like me worked for him. He promised me a promotion, but when the time came, he handed the promotion to one of his acquaintances.

Why the Parable?

- We must be prepared for any eventuality.
- We must keep our lamps burning brightly.
- It will take heart, mind and intuition working together to avoid mishaps.
- We must wait, be patient and anticipate.
- We must be ready to open the door the moment we hear a knock.
- We must remain vigilant at all times; and
- We must not fall asleep.

* * * * *

Related Parables

1. We Must Be Ready

"Stay dressed for action and keep your lamps burning, and be like men who are waiting for their master to come home from the wedding feast, so that they may open the door to him at once when he comes and knocks. Blessed are those servants whom the master finds awake when he comes. Truly, I say to you, he will dress himself for service and have them recline at table, and he will come and serve them. If he comes in the second watch, or in the third, and finds them awake, blessed are those servants! But know this, that if the master of the house had known at what hour the thief was coming, he would not have left his house to be broken into. You also must be ready, for the Son of Man is coming at an hour you do not expect." Luke 12:35-40

Dressed for action

We must dress (mentally prepare), not only for success, but for whatever the occasion calls for. Dressed for action means having the mental fortitude to face any situation that we are confronted with. It means always being ready.

Lamps burning

Our lamps must be like eternal fires never dimming their light. Our light is the flame of the Inner Spiritual Self imbued with the Christ Consciousness.

Waiting, anticipating

We must remain alert, not allowing an opportunity to slip by where we could make a positive impact.

Ready to open the door

Opportunity can knock at any time, especially when least expected. We must be ready to open the door as soon as we hear the knock.

Dressed for service

Being ready and willing to serve is among the greatest of Christian virtues. Christ told us that the greatest among us is the one who serves the most. Service is thought out and rendered to empower, not to create dependencies.

Staying awake

No dozing off. No sleeping on the job. Eyes wide open. Ears clear and attentive. Hearts alert with anticipation.

What does it mean to be ready and awake?

We are students in the school of life. A test might come at any moment. If we have been studying and are prepared, we do not have to fear the exams. We welcome them to prove our metal. Like Christ who was ready and triumphed when Satan tempted and tested Him, we will be triumphant if we stay awake, are prepared and ready.

2. Watch Yourselves

"But watch yourselves lest your hearts be weighed down with dissipation and drunkenness and cares of this life, and that day come upon you suddenly like a trap. For it will come upon all who dwell on the face of the whole earth. But stay awake at all times, praying that you may have strength to escape all these things that are going to take place, and to stand before the Son of Man." Luke 21:34-36

Hearts weighted down

It is easy for our hearts to be weighed down. There is so much to worry about and to grieve over. We have many burdens that we must bear, some of our own making and others dumped on us through circumstance. We carry the heavy load of our many duties, obligations and responsibilities.

Dissipation

It is easy to dissipate our time, energy and other resources over the many things that need to be done. Yet, we must prioritize. 80% of what demands our time is trivia. Why not concentrate on doing the vital 20% and ignoring the trivial 80%?

Drunkenness

To be drunk is to function with our faculties impaired. We must avoid getting drunk. We must stay sober and act with full mental, physical and spiritual capacity for best results.

Cares

Cares are like germs that infest our minds and hearts. Too many cares cause stress and tension that can lead to disease. We can live without being overwhelmed by these cares. We can inoculate ourselves against cares that infest with the vaccines of trust, confidence, faith and inner strength.

This is the fate of everyone

> *"For it will come upon all who dwell on the face of the whole earth."*

Being human, we will face challenges, have difficulties, experience heartaches and feel disappointed. Yet, we are not victims and should never give in and act as if we are. We have a lamp within that will guide us out of any morass if we seek its guidance and follow its promptings.

Stay awake

This admonition is repeated several times. Stay awake. Do not fall asleep. Be vigilant. Keep your wits about you.

3. Build Your House on Rock

> *"Why do you call me 'Lord, Lord,' and not do what I tell you? Everyone who comes to me and hears my words and does them, I will show you what he is like: he is like a man building a house, who dug deep and laid the foundation on the rock. And when a flood arose, the stream broke against that house and could not shake it, because it had been well built. But the one who hears and does not do them is like a man who built a house on the ground without a foundation. When the stream broke against it, immediately it fell, and the ruin of that house was great."*
> Luke 6:46-49

House

Our house is our life. We need to build a life that we feel at home with. Some build castles while others are happy with a hut. Whatever we build must have a strong, stable foundation.

Digging deep

We must dig deep to lay down a strong, steady, unshakeable foundation. This foundation is confidence in our abilities founded on knowledge accumulated from our diverse experiences.

The Rock

Rocks are symbols for solidity, steadfastness and endurance. Our rock is our faith in ourselves and the divine within. Our faith is our deep-rooted conviction that we matter and that we can make a difference. The disciple Peter, whose name means "rock" is a symbolic representation of this deep-rooted faith. Christ did not build His church on Peter. He built it on rock solid faith and conviction exemplified by Peter. Hence, faith is the key, not the person.

> *He said to them, "But who do you say that I am?" Simon Peter replied, "You are the Christ, the Son of the living God." And Jesus answered him, "Blessed are you, Simon Bar-Jonah! For flesh and blood has not revealed this to you, but my Father who is in heaven. And I tell you, you are Peter, and on this rock I will build my church, and the gates of hell shall not prevail against it. Matt 16:15-18*

Floods

Floods are the unexpected challenges life throws at us. If our house is not built on a solid foundation, floods can destroy our "house"— our normal life. We can withstand any difficulty if we have a strong faith and confidence in ourselves.

Action is the critical factor

> *"But the one who hears and does not do them is like a man who built a house on the ground without a*

foundation."

Hearing and not acting is useless. Believing and not expressing is powerless. We cannot be productive unless we act.

4. A rock-solid foundation consists of faith and action.

"What good is it, my brothers, if someone says he has faith but does not have works? Can that faith save him? If a brother or sister is poorly clothed and lacking in daily food, and one of you says to them, "Go in peace, be warmed and filled," without giving them the things needed for the body, what good is that? So also faith by itself, if it does not have works, is dead." James 2:14-17

Well said.

PARABLE OF THE TALENTS

Your talent is God's gift to you. What you do with it is your gift back to God. —Leo Buscaglia

The Parable

(a talent was a monetary unit worth about twenty years' wages for a laborer)

"For it will be like a man going on a journey, who called his servants and entrusted to them his property. To one he gave five talents to another two, to another one, to each according to his ability. Then he went away. He who had received the five talents went at once and traded with them, and he made five talents more. So also he who had the two talents made two talents more. But he who had received the one talent went and dug in the ground and hid his master's money. Now after a long time the master of those servants came and settled accounts with them. And he who had received the five talents came forward, bringing five talents more, saying, 'Master, you delivered to me five talents; here I have made five talents more.' His master said to him, 'Well done, good and faithful servant. You have been faithful over a little; I will set you over much. Enter into the joy of your master.' And he also who had the two talents came forward, saying, 'Master, *you delivered to me two talents; here I have made two talents more.' His master said to him, 'Well done, good and faithful servant. You have been faithful over a little; I will set you over much. Enter into the joy of your master.' He also who had received the one talent came forward, saying, 'Master, I knew you to be a hard man, reaping where you did not sow, and gathering where you scattered no seed, so I was afraid, and I went and hid your talent in the ground. Here you have what is yours.' But his master answered him, 'You wicked and slothful servant! You knew that I reap where I have not sown and gather where I scattered no seed? Then you ought to have invested my money with the bankers, and at my coming I should have received what was my own with interest. So take the talent from him and give it to him who has the ten talents. For to everyone who has will more be given, and he will have an abundance. But from the one who has not, even what he has will be taken away. And cast the worthless servant into the outer darkness. In that place there will be weeping and gnashing of teeth.' Matt 25: 14-30*

The Hidden Meaning

Talents

It is apparent from this parable that we are all given talents, some more than others. Some are given one, others two and a few five talents. Those with more talents, however, have a larger responsibility. These talents are gifts from life. Our "talents" could be wealth, status, inheritance, skills and abilities. This is what we start with as seed investment. We are informed that each is given according to his or her ability. The good news is that regardless of how many talents with start with, how many we end up with is up to us. We determine our rate of return. The higher the rate, the more talents we end up with. In other words, our return depends on how good of an investor we are and the tools and techniques we employ.

We are born with certain tendencies and proclivities. These are the "talents" that we have to work with. We can add to these as we live, learn and grow. Initially, our talents are as seeds lying dormant in our genes. If we learn to develop and express these talents, then we will reap an abundance of returns. In other words, within us lies the potential for greatness. We need to awaken and activate these seeds of greatness so they can blossom and become majestic "trees" yielding an abundance of "fruit".

Going on a journey

When the master (our employer) is gone, we are on our own. We have no supervision. In other words, unless we are internally motivated to act, nothing will be achieved. To excel requires personal initiative to go beyond what is expected of us. The natural tendency is inaction due to inertia—the path of least resistance. We must overcome our inertia and find a reason to accomplish whatever we would like to achieve. We can do this by visualizing the end result of our effort. We can feel what it would be once we attain what our hearts desire.

Trust and entrusting

The talents that we consider to be ours, are in reality, entrusted to us. We are the trustees holding these gifts in trust, not to hide or keep them idle, but to use them as germinating seeds to multiply the return on our investment. These are our mustard seeds, yeast, pearl, treasure and net that Christ alluded to. With these we can transform our lives and impact the lives of the many.

The one who did not invest

The person with one talent had the least. It was expected that this individual would work the hardest. Instead, this person dug a hole and buried his talent unused. These types of individuals decline to invest in themselves and cultivate their innate capabilities. They are overtaken by fear, worry and uncertainty. They are mostly in survival mode, living day-to-day, seeking treasures that are material and temporary. They lack the vision for a brighter future, do not exercise free will and are guided solely by the ego. Living to survive makes these individuals no better than the beasts. Their precious resources are wasted on entertainment and meeting the cares, burdens and responsibilities of life.

The servant with the one talent hid his talent in the ground because he was afraid and unsure of himself. Fear and uncertainty are real and we must learn how to deal with them. Most fears stem from lack of confidence while uncertainty is due to inexperience. Hence, the more prepared we are, the less fearful we will be and the more we will act with confidence, thus becoming more confident. With experience, we become more sure of ourselves and less fearful of undesirable consequences. The master's message for this servant is: "Use it or lose it." This is true not only with talents, skills and abilities, but also with our muscles and neurons. What we use, we enhance. What we ignore, slowly but surely atrophies.

The one who doubled the two talents

This servant is diligent, conscientious and knows that he has been entrusted with something valuable that he must put to good use. Given two talents to start with, he is aware that by the end of his life, he has to account for his gifts. From this parable, it is evident that we are expected to at least double what we initially start with. Since this servant doubled the return on his investment, he was lauded by the master. In life, to significantly increase the return on our investment is to be a skilled tool user. The best tools to use are mental. These include imagination, visualization, meditation, prayer, concentration, contemplation and cooperation with others.

The one who doubled the five talents

This servant was the most successful. Even though the rate of return was still a mere doubling of his initial investment, he had much more that needed to be doubled. This servant knew how to live guided by the Voice Within. His main focus in life was on the vital 20% ignoring the remaining trivial 80%. He sought that which does not spoil—the spiritual aspect of living—learning, loving, serving and empowering. The motto of this servant was: "Thy will be done." In addition to being a skilled mental tool user, this individual was adept at using the spiritual tools of intuition, inspiration and creativity. This servant seldom worked alone. He employed the master-mind concept where he cooperated with others of like mind, where they gave of themselves joyously, pooling their resources and abilities for the maximum benefit for all.

Faithful over the little

For those who have been faithful over the little that has been entrusted to them, much more will be given. They have earned it through their diligence, intelligent decisions and actions.

The master returns

When the master returns, it is time to show what we have done with our gifts. Usually, this takes place after death when we are back in the spirit world and where we face our own Inner Spiritual Self and review our lives. This is the day of reckoning. This is what the ancient Egyptians called "the Hall of Justice" where our "soul" is weighed against the feather of truth, MAAT. Those who pass the test are rewarded by being given a new chance to enter the world for a fresh set of challenges and opportunities to learn and grow. Those who fail the test, the punishment is simply stagnation and a repetition of what they have already gone through before.

This judgment hall is ever-present for these spiritually awake individuals. Their conscience as judge is ever vigilant. These individuals know the consequences of their actions immediately. If they do anything wrong, they take action to remedy the situation. Their conscience is their judge.

Consequences

Life is a trading post where we are expected to engage in it for a profit. We earn the best return on our investments when we use our talents to seek knowledge and spiritual growth—treasures that do not spoil. Life is a vineyard where we are expected to change ordinary grapes into delectable wine. If we do, then we have succeeded in our mission. If we do not, there is no judgment or punishment, but there are consequences that we must live with. Life is not easy. We will face difficulties and challenges. These must be transmuted into opportunities for learning, growth and for making a positive contribution.

Talents, skills and abilities are like seeds. Unplanted and unnurtured seeds do not give any returns. They remain dormant. A "master farmer" does not like dormant seeds. Seeds are for planting, growing and yielding an abundance. The "master farmer" will take away the unplanted seeds from the unproductive and give them to the those who can produce the best returns.

We are expected to be productive.

Personalizing the Parable

Too much money and wealth are not easy to manage. They create many challenges that can lead to worry, stress and loss of focus. That is why Christ said:

> *Again I tell you, it is easier for a camel to go through the eye of a needle than for a rich person to enter the kingdom of God." Matt 19:24*

This is not because there is anything wrong with money or wealth. Wealth can be all-consuming and becomes the number one priority of our lives resulting in loss of focus about what is really important. Instead of us being the masters of our wealth, it becomes the ruler of our lives. The ideal situation would be to strive for enough material goods to have a comfortable life and then devote our resources to acquire knowledge and to grow spiritually. Obviously, each must decide what is enough to make them feel comfortable.

The most valuable wealth we have are talents, skills and abilities. These are hidden treasures buried deep within and are transforming agents that can alter not only our present, but shape our future as well.

There are three ways to live. We can seek worldly pleasures and make these our focus and priority. This is the default choice for most. Unless we knowingly, intentionally and willingly decide to choose a different mode of living, the default mode will take hold. We will live solely for the material and seek only that which does not endure. We become like the Prodigal Son who immersed himself in the world and forgot his heritage. We can live like him and frolic with the swine. This is an option for the many and if we are happy with the consequences, then there is nothing wrong with our choice.

The second option is to live a balanced life where we have enough material goods for a comfortable life and then focus on the spiritual aspects of life. This is an easy choice because it does not call for any sacrifices. The return on this investment could be as high as fivefold. The individual, in this case, lives a moderate, balanced life using his or her faculties to advance his or her station in life.

The third option is to live a totally spiritual life—a life of service following the example of Christ. This is not an easy choice and very few opt for this option. The yield on this type of living is at least tenfold. This is a choice we can opt for later on after we retire.

We go through three main stages in life. In the first stage, we are dependent on our parents. Our focus is growth and the acquisition of knowledge via continued education.

In the second stage, we work, raise a family and build up our reserves for a comfortable retirement.

The third stage is when we retire. Now we have the freedom to pursue anything we desire. Most have the time and are comfortable resource-wise to do what they like. This is the best opportunity to seek knowledge and to grow spiritually. Retirement is an incredibly valuable gift that we must manage wisely. Yes, we can play golf all day or do whatever else we like. But is this a wise investment of our time? Why not allocate some time to seek treasures that do not spoil—knowledge and spiritual growth?

Why the Parable?

"Talents" are any resource we can invest for a return—money, time, skills, abilities and even our contacts and connections.

- We are expected to invest the resources we are entrusted with.
- The return on our investment is up to us. We are expected to at least double the return on our investment by the end of our lives.
- If we are diligent and show a good return, we will end up with even more.
- Otherwise, we will lose even the little we now have.
- The motto "use it or lose it" is a good one to keep in mind.
- The best policy to ensure a good return is to provide the best service.
- Idleness, or no action, is not an acceptable option and is not tolerated.

- We must be skilled tool users to increase the return on our investment.
- The best tools to use are mental and spiritual—imagination, visualization, concentration, contemplation, meditation, prayer, intuition, inspiration and listening to the Voice Within.

The Parable from Other Sources

The parable of the Ten Minas (Luke)

(a mina was about three months' wages for a laborer)
As they heard these things, he proceeded to tell a parable, because he was near to Jerusalem, and because they supposed that the kingdom of God was to appear immediately. He said therefore, "A nobleman went into a far country to receive for himself a kingdom and then return. Calling ten of his servants, he gave them ten minas, and said to them, 'Engage in business until I come.' But his citizens hated him and sent a delegation after him, saying, 'We do not want this man to reign over us.' When he returned, having received the kingdom, he ordered these servants to whom he had given the money to be called to him, that he might know what they had gained by doing business. The first came before him, saying, 'Lord, your mina has made ten minas more.' And he said to him, 'Well done, good servant! Because you have been faithful in a very little, you shall have authority over ten cities.' And the second came, saying, 'Lord, your mina has made five minas.' And he said to him, 'And you are to be over five cities.' Then another came, saying, 'Lord, here is your mina, which I kept laid away in a handkerchief; for I was afraid of you, because you are a severe man. You take what you did not deposit, and reap what you did not sow.' He said to him, 'I will condemn you with your own

words, you wicked servant! You knew that I was a severe man, taking what I did not deposit and reaping what I did not sow? Why then did you not put my money in the bank, and at my coming I might have collected it with interest?' And he said to those who stood by, 'Take the mina from him, and give it to the one who has the ten minas.' And they said to him, 'Lord, he has ten minas!' 'I tell you that to everyone who has, more will be given, but from the one who has not, even what he has will be taken away. But as for these enemies of mine, who did not want me to reign over them, bring them here and slaughter them before me.'" Luke 19:11-27

This is a similar parable to that given in Matthew. The difference is that 10 servants are given 1 mina each and the returns on the investments are different.

One of the servants uses the 1 mina to earn fivefold. Another uses the 1 mina for a tenfold return. The rate of return is entirely up to us based on our investment skills and the tools and techniques we employ. The return on our investment should grow as we become more proficient. Once more, idleness or inaction is not tolerated.

PARABLE OF THE GOOD SAMARITAN

Those who bring sunshine into the lives of others cannot keep it from themselves. —James M. Barrie

The Parable

And behold, a lawyer stood up to put him to the test, saying, "Teacher, what shall I do to inherit eternal life?" He said to him, "What is written in the Law? How do you read it?" And he answered, "You shall love the Lord your God with all your heart and with all your soul and with all your strength and with all your mind, and your neighbor as yourself." And he said to him, "You have answered correctly; do this, and you will live."

But he, desiring to justify himself, said to Jesus, "And who is my neighbor?" Jesus replied, "A man was going down from Jerusalem to Jericho, and he fell among robbers, who stripped him and beat him and departed, leaving him half dead. Now by chance a priest was going down that road, and when he saw him he passed by on the other side. So likewise a Levite, when he came to the place and saw him, passed by on the other side. But a Samaritan, as he journeyed, came to where he was, and when he saw him, he had compassion. He went to him and bound up his wounds, pouring on oil and wine. Then he set him on his own animal and brought him to an inn and took care of him. And the next day he took out two denarii and gave them to the innkeeper, saying, 'Take care of him, and whatever more you spend, I will repay you when I come back.' Which of these three, do you think, proved to be a neighbor to the man who fell among the robbers?" He said, "The one who showed him mercy." And Jesus said to him, "You go, and do likewise." Luke 10:25-37

The Hidden Meaning

A lawyer puts Christ to the test

A lawyer wants to test Christ so he asks Him a tricky question. *"Teacher, what shall I do to inherit eternal life?"* Christ does not fall for the trap. Instead, He asks the lawyer: *"What is written in the Law? How do you read it?"* In other words, you tell me what your religion teaches you to do and do it.

A priest

A priest is someone expected to be devout, pious and helpful. The priest preaches mercy to others yet when he encounters the injured traveler, he pretends not to see him and walks over to the other side.

A Levite

A Levite is someone who serves religious functions. Just like the priest, instead of practicing what he preaches, he, too ignores the injured traveler and walks to the other side, perhaps to avoid eye contact.

A Samaritan

A Samaritan is not expected to stop and help the injured traveler perhaps because the injured traveler is a Jew while he is a Samaritan. Jews and Samaritans did not relate with each other since Samaritans were a racially mixed society, many with pagan ancestry.

Yet, it is the one who is not expected to show mercy that does exactly that. The Samaritan was moved by compassion. He binds the injured man's wounds pouring oil and wine over them. He set the injured man on his own animal. In other words, the Samaritan walked while the injured man rode the animal. He took the injured traveler to an inn and set him up to rest and recover. He, not only paid the inn keeper two denarii, but promised to come back, check on the injured traveler and settle any outstanding bills.

Who is our neighbor?

Once more Christ does not tell the lawyer who was neighborly, but asks him to answer the question: *Which of these three, do you think, proved to be a neighbor to the man who fell among the robbers?"* When the lawyer answered: The one who showed mercy, Christ told him to do likewise.

In this parable, Christ is emphasizing the absence of class or racial distinction. People who show compassion distinguish themselves and become favored by God. No more pre-favoring one group of people over another via labels such as "The Chosen People." Our acts distinguish us one from another.

Going beyond what is expected

The Samaritan, not only brought the injured man to the inn, but, "the next day he took out two denarii and gave them to the innkeeper, saying, "Take care of him, and whatever more you spend, I will repay you when I come back."' This is going beyond what is expected. This Samaritan is a true Christian after Christ's heart. Through this parable Christ is emphasizing His New teachings— the complete break away from the Old way of living:

"You have heard that it was said, 'An eye for an eye and a tooth for a tooth.' But I say to you, Do not resist the one who is evil. But if anyone slaps you on the right cheek, turn to him the other also. And

if anyone would sue you and take your tunic, let him have your cloak as well. And if anyone forces you to go one mile, go with him two miles. Give to the one who begs from you, and do not refuse the one who would borrow from you. Matt 5:38-42

Am I my brother's keeper?

The question is often asked: "Am I my brother's keeper?" We are all each other's keepers. We need each other. We go through various stages in life. At times, we are down and vulnerable and could use some assistance. At other times, we are up and are in a position to render assistance to someone who needs it. Life is cyclic. What goes up can come down and what is down can go up. Taking care of each other should not feel like a responsibility, but an occasion for joyful service.

Personalizing the Parable

It is interesting that the traveler was on a journey, just like the priest, the Levite and the Samaritan. We are on a journey as well. Our journey is through life and on this journey we will encounter many who could use our assistance. How would we act? Would we move to the other side of the road and pretend not to notice? Or, would we do what it takes to help the person get back on his or her feet?

My life is shaped, not as much by what I did, but also by what others did. At several junctures in my life when I needed assistance the most, someone was there to lend me a helping hand. I am eternally thankful for those compassionate individuals whose generosity not only touched my life, but showed me what a privilege it is to be in a position to assist someone else. We should feel blessed if we can help another. Obviously, we must know that we are indeed helping someone and not carelessly giving, creating dependencies, encouraging laziness or feeding an addiction.

What is spirituality?

Spirituality is looking at everyone as members of our family. We have one Father. We have one source and we all share the same destiny. However, each is on a different path and at various distances along their journey of life. Each has unique challenges to face, lessons to learn and contributions to make.

The purpose of this parable is that we should emulate the Good Samaritan who did his noble deed anonymously, without seeking praise or recognition.

> *"Thus, when you give to the needy, sound no trumpet before you, as the hypocrites do in the synagogues and in the streets, that they may be praised by others. Truly, I say to you, they have received their reward. But when you give to the needy, do not let your left hand know what your right hand is doing, so that your giving may be in secret. And your Father who sees in secret will reward you. Matt 6:2-4*

We should do likewise.

Why the Parable

This parable is straight forward and does not require much explaining. But why is Christ telling us this parable?

Gone are the days when we look at others as friend or foe, as my kin or strangers. Gone are the days when we act without care and compassion. The days of Old are over. A new age has dawned upon us—an age of love, compassion, caring and lending a helping hand. Gone are the days of the commandments where every aspect of our lives is controlled. We have only one commandment and this commandment is not externally imposed upon us. It is an internal outpouring of love, mercy and caring from the depth our hearts.

This parable is another example of emphasizing that we are

no longer under the Law:

> *For sin will have no dominion over you, since you are not under law but under grace. Rom 6:14*

So, who is our neighbor?

Our neighbor is anyone and everyone we encounter who could use our assistance. Our neighbor is literally the ones closest to us, the ones in our immediate environment. We do not have to concern ourselves with what we do not have an immediate influence over. Our work begins right where we are. Most of what we need to do is in front of us staring us in the face.

A Note Regarding Samaritans

Reading the Bible can be confusing and at times even contradictory. Here is an example regarding the Samaritans:

> *These twelve Jesus sent out, instructing them, "Go nowhere among the Gentiles and enter no town of the Samaritans, Matt 10:5*

Yet, in the next quote, we realize that the disciples did indeed go to the Samaritans.

> *Now when they had testified and spoken the word of the Lord, they returned to Jerusalem, preaching the gospel to many villages of the Samaritans. Acts 8:25*

Jesus Himself cleanses 10 lepers from Samaria:

> *On the way to Jerusalem he was passing along between Samaria and Galilee. And as he entered a village, he was met by ten lepers, who stood at a distance and lifted up their voices, saying, "Jesus, Master, have mercy on us." When he saw them he said to them, "Go and show yourselves to the priests." And as they went they were*

cleansed. Then one of them, when he saw that he was healed, turned back, praising God with a loud voice; and he fell on his face at Jesus' feet, giving him thanks. Now he was a Samaritan. Then Jesus answered, "Were not ten cleansed? Where are the nine? Was no one found to return and give praise to God except this foreigner?" And he said to him, "Rise and go your way; your faith has made you well." Luke 17:11-19

Another important example of a Samaritan in the New Testament is that of the Samaritan woman:

A woman from Samaria came to draw water. Jesus said to her, "Give me a drink." (For his disciples had gone away into the city to buy food.) The Samaritan woman said to him, "How is it that you, a Jew, ask for a drink from me, a woman of Samaria?" (For Jews have no dealings with Samaritans.) John 4:7-9

Many Samaritans from that town believed in him because of the woman's testimony, "He told me all that I ever did." So when the Samaritans came to him, they asked him to stay with them, and he stayed there two days. And many more believed because of his word. They said to the woman, "It is no longer because of what you said that we believe, for we have heard for ourselves, and we know that this is indeed the Savior of the world." John 4:39-42

On another occasion Jesus Himself was accused of being a Samaritan:

The Jews answered him, "Are we not right in saying that you are a Samaritan and have a demon?" John 8:48

Reading the Bible, we might get contradictory messages and that is understandable. The writings are not by eye witnesses or contemporaries of Christ. They are oral traditions that were written down decades after the fact. None of the writers knew Christ personally or heard Him speak.

Even though the statements in the Bible can be contradictory, the parables are much more reliable to glean Christ's teachings. The parables are stories embodying the essence of the teachings of Christ. Their message is unambiguous, straightforward and preserved for all generations to read and unravel the hidden messages buried within.

And that is the purpose of this book.

PARABLE OF THE FRIEND AT MIDNIGHT

The table of elements does not contain one of the most powerful elements that make up our world, and that is the element of surprise. —Daniel Handler

The Parable

And he said to them, "Which of you who has a friend will go to him at midnight and say to him, 'Friend, lend me three loaves, for a friend of mine has arrived on a journey, and I have nothing to set before him'; and he will answer from within, 'Do not bother me; the door is now shut, and my children are with me in bed. I cannot get up and give you anything'? I tell you, though he will not get up and give him anything because he is his friend, yet because of his impudence he will rise and give him whatever he needs. And I tell you, ask, and it will be given to you; seek, and you will find; knock, and it will be opened to you. For everyone who asks receives, and the one who seeks finds, and to the one who knocks it will be opened. What father among you, if his son asks for a fish, will instead of a fish give him a serpent; or if he asks for an egg, will give him a scorpion? If you then, who are evil, know how to give good gifts to your children, how much more will the heavenly Father give the Holy Spirit to those who ask him!" Luke 11:5-13

The Hidden Meaning

3 loaves of bread

Three is a mystical number denoting creativity, multiplicity and growth. Loaves of bread are essentials we need for a healthy life. In this parable, Christ is indicating that to have what we need and to have it abundantly requires creativity. Christ is the bread of life. In other words, the nutrition we need is spiritual because we do not live by bread alone, but by the spiritual teachings embedded in the parables of Christ.

Friend at midnight

No one in real life would go to a friend's house at midnight asking for anything. In this parable, midnight is when the unexpected happens. Unexpected emergencies are part of life and everyone experiences them. Those who are prepared will fare better.

A friend's visit at midnight is not an emergency. Should a real emergency happen, instead of panicking, Christ is reminding us to treat the emergency as a friend. In other words, we need to see the emergency as an opportunity. To do this, we need to calm down, breathe slowly and deeply, detach and see the bigger picture from above.

Impudence

Normally, if a friend visits us at midnight and asks us for something, we would not get up and open the door. But because of the impudence of that friend, we will get up and give that friend what he or she needs. Creativity is required when we are in a bind and are in need of a solution. Impudence is insolence, boldness and nerve. We cannot be timid in the face of challenges. We have to face them head-on and deal with the situation with courage and tenacity. We must do what it takes to solve our problem. If impudence is what is needed, then so be it. By overcoming our challenges, we learn, grow and enhance our confidence.

> *"For everyone who asks receives, and the one who seeks finds, and to the one who knocks it will be opened." Luke 11:10*

Seek, knock and ask

These are active, action verbs. It is up to us to seek, knock and ask if we want something. The cosmic is listening and will respond only if we know how to seek, where to knock and who to ask. We must gird ourselves with boldness and nerve. Our seeking must be in earnest. Our knocking must be loud and persistent and our asking must be direct. Who we ask is our Inner Spiritual Self, the Christ Consciousness within who will guide us to the solution we need.

Fish or serpent. Egg or scorpion.

If we ask sincerely, then what we get is in the image of what we ask for. We can ask for what we need such as fish or eggs but it is far better to ask for the knowledge and the skills required to earn what we need and create it ourselves. Asking for guidance, wisdom, knowledge and understanding are much more valuable than asking for temporary goods that satisfy for today only. Why not seek permanent skills instead that will alter the trajectory of our lives? Solving our own problems is a sign of maturity.

Symbolically, fish is food. What we need is both types of nourishment—food for the body and food for the soul. If we ask for material fish, we sustain the body for a day. If we ask for spiritual food, we renew and regenerate the spiritual body and we are resurrected from spiritual death.

Serpent is a symbol of regeneration, renewal, death and resurrection.

Eggs are perhaps the most consumed food item the world over. Imagine all the eggs that cruise ships, restaurants and homes use daily. Eggs are symbolic of the life principle, concentrated potential and undifferentiated "stem cells" that can grow into anything. Eggs are the source of creation and creativity. We can ask for physical eggs or for spiritual eggs—the opportunity to manifest our vast innate potential.

Scorpions are symbolic of death and destruction. We do not want these in our lives. However, if we encounter them in the form of a disaster, then we must convert them into allies and friends. We can learn from them. We can redirect the trajectory of our lives and chart a new course because of them. Having experienced disaster, we can live preventive lives in the future.

Difficulties are "friends at midnight."

Difficulties and challenges are uninvited guests. They appear at "midnight" unexpectedly and demand our attention. Instead of fearing them and getting bent out-of-shape, why not look at them as opportunities for growth? It is only by overcoming challenges and facing difficulties that we grow and mature. Encountering challenges at "midnight" are an essential component of a normal and healthy life.

Just-in-time solutions

If we are attuned to the Voice Within and are open to intuition and inspiration, then just-in-time solutions will appear and we will know what to do next. If we are facing a crisis and we do not know how to proceed, then this is the time to seek earnestly, knock boldly and ask passionately. We should include our heart and mind when we seek, knock and ask. The answer will appear just as Christ promised. It will appear suddenly, unexpectedly and in ways that might surprise us.

Personalizing the Parable

The most powerful tools we have at our disposal are advanced mental tools such as visualization, imagination, meditation, prayer, contemplation and concentration. Cultivating these, and mastering their use will provide us with shortcuts to attain our goals and hearts' desires in the quickest and most efficient way.

We can seek, knock and ask for anything we like. However, what comes back to us is often what we need and not what we want. Our job is to do the asking, knocking and seeking. Then we let go without demanding what the outcome should be. Our Inner Spiritual Self knows what is best for us. Our motto should always be: "Thy will be done," the will of the Inner Spiritual Self rather than the will of the ego.

The gift of the Holy Spirit

> *"If you then, who are evil, know how to give good gifts to your children, how much more will the heavenly Father give the Holy Spirit to those who ask him!" Luke 11:13*

If we are fortunate when we seek, knock and ask, our heavenly Father will not give us what we want; rather, we will have the gift of the Holy Spirit. And what is the Holy Spirit? It is what descended on Jesus during His baptism and He realized who He was—a child of God.

The Holy Spirit is what descended on the disciples and they had all sorts of knowledge, skills and abilities. The gift of the Holy Spirit is the best gift of all. It gives us the knowledge to solve our own problems and the wisdom to transform our challenges into opportunities.

Why the Parable?

- Life is full of surprises.
- We will face challenges and encounter difficulties.

- We must face our challenges with boldness and nerve.
- At times, we must be impudent.
- If we seek in earnest, knock boldly and ask with passion, a door will open for us.
- What we receive is often in the image of what we ask for.
- It is better to receive what we need rather than what we want.
- The gift of the Holy spirit is the best gift we can ever have.

PARABLE OF THE RICH FOOL

The fool sees naught but folly; and the madman only madness. Yesterday I asked a foolish man to count the fools among us. He laughed and said, "This is too hard a thing to do, and it will take too long. Were it not better to count only the wise?" —Khalil Gibran

The Parable

Someone in the crowd said to him, "Teacher, tell my brother to divide the inheritance with me." But he said to him, "Man, who made me a judge or arbitrator over you?" And he said to them, "Take care, and be on your guard against all covetousness, for one's life does not consist in the abundance of his possessions." And he told them a parable, saying, "The land of a rich man produced plentifully, and he thought to himself, 'What shall I do, for I have nowhere to store my crops?' And he said, 'I will do this: I will tear down my barns and build larger ones, and there I will store all my grain and my goods. And I will say to my soul, "Soul, you have ample goods laid up for many years; relax, eat, drink, be merry."' But God said to him, 'Fool! This night your soul is required of you, and the things you have prepared, whose will they be?' So is the one who lays up treasure for himself and is not rich toward God." Luke 12:13-21

The Hidden Meaning

Judging and judgment

Not judging others is an important message of Christ. He never judged anyone and when asked to play a judge in the case of this parable, He refused. *"Man, who made me a judge or arbitrator over you?"* is a wonderful advice we should keep in mind. The only one we can judge is ourselves. And this should be an examination. Many believe that there is a final judgment day and that God will either put us in heaven or throw us to eternal fire and damnation. This is a human invention to gain control over us through fear. The God I know is a God of Love through and through. This God does not have any human qualities such as the need for punishment or the desire for judgment. After death, we are in spirit form. We review our actions, evaluate their consequences and become wiser as a result. The purpose of living is experiencing so our eyes open and we know who we really are in essence. Only the physical body with its nervous system can experience pain and suffering. Since the body disintegrates after we die and is no more, who or what will suffer in hell for eternity? If Christ does not judge anyone, neither should we judge others. Instead of judging, perhaps we should learn to be tolerant and understanding. We should always remember the log in our eyes before we point to the speck in someone else's eye.

Covetousness

Greed is wanting more and more. It is having no limits or boundaries. It is a lack of appreciation for what we already have. Greed is a vice for a good reason. It is due to our misplaced focus. Being greedy is being ever hungry for more and never being satisfied. Being greedy is not knowing when we have enough. Greed is not the same as ambition. Ambition is a virtue. Through ambition we seek to improve the quality of our lives. The best way to improve our lives is to add to our skill set and increase our knowledge.

Quality of life does not depend on possessions

We never possess anything. We are mere custodians of what we have and own. All of our "possessions" are temporary. They age and deteriorate and ultimately, we part from them when we die. Being custodians, we take care of them, enjoy them and do not get attached to them. The quality of our lives does not depend on what we own. We can have a wonderful life with a little or with a lot. The quality of our lives mostly depends on our mental attitude. We can enjoy and appreciate the free gifts of nature without ever owning them—sunrises, sunsets, flowers, animals, waterfalls, clouds, rain and snow. Additionally, the most important contributor to the quality of our lives is close, loving and intimate relationships. These, too, are free.

Storing goods that do not endure

The rich man had plenty to be satisfied with. He wanted more to assure his wellbeing into the far future. Believing that he would live for many more years, he built bigger and better storage rooms. Yet, his soul left him that same night.

Christ's message in this parable is clear:

"Do not lay up for yourselves treasures on earth, where moth and rust destroy and where thieves break in and steal, but lay up for yourselves treasures in heaven, where neither moth nor rust destroys and where thieves do not break in and steal. For where your treasure is, there your heart will be also. Matt 6:19-21

This does not mean that we should not plan for the future. We can and we should. However, we must never neglect what is even more important—doing our best right here and right now to enrich our minds and souls.

We should always keep in mind that we could die at any moment.

Relax, eat, drink and be merry

For many, life is about eating, drinking and being merry. These are important contributors to the enjoyment of life but they cannot be all we do. We must allocate time and energy to pursue what is even more important—treasures that endure. Life must be balanced. If all we do is seek material pleasure, then we miss out on the most important—cultivating our minds and enriching our souls. We can derive pleasure from a variety of sources—beauty in nature and in people, music, the arts, reading, writing, learning, a walk in the park, intimacy and creativity.

The time of our death is unknown

We live on borrowed time. To live as if we will never die is foolish. Not knowing when our end will come, it is wise to live as if it can happen at any moment. Hence, our house should always be in order. Being ready and prepared eliminates the impact of surprises. Additionally, if our house is in order when we do die, we leave less for our loved ones to deal with.

Treasures of Earth and those of Heaven

Treasures of earth are those that moth and rust destroy and where thieves break in and steal. Treasures of earth are external and can be seen. They are temporary. Treasures of heaven are internal and spiritual. They are accessible only through vision and imagination. These treasures are permanent aspects of who we are, our character and personality. They embody our sublimated thoughts, habits, attitudes, expectations, beliefs, and knowledge.

Personalizing the Parable

What makes life worthwhile?

1. Appreciating beauty.
2. Being in love.
3. Experiencing Joy.
4. Discovery, travel and adventure.
5. Touching lives, learning, teaching, empowering and helping.
6. Quality family relationships and intimacy.
7. Being a lighthouse dispelling darkness.

These are treasures we should seek. We do not need a storage place to keep these since they do not require space. These treasures are internal and we can access them and enjoy them anytime we like. It is important to remember Christ's adage: *'Fool! This night your soul is required of you, and the things you have prepared, whose will they be?'*

Keeping this in mind, it behooves us to learn to prioritize and do what is important first, always doing what we can right away without delay. No postponement or procrastination. If not now, then when? Trivia and distractions can take over our lives. We must avoid these by doing the important things first. *"Defer not till the evening what the morning may accomplish."* **Unto Thee I Grant.** Obviously, if we need more information before we can act, then we should wait. Otherwise, we should act right away.

Why the Parable?

- We could die at any moment.
- Our house should be in order at all times.
- Possessions are not an index of happiness.
- We should seek treasures that do not spoil.
- Greed does not pay.

- There are many simple things we can enjoy for free.
- We must discriminate between what is valuable and what is not.

Gospel of Thomas

There was a rich man who had considerable wealth. He said, "I will use my money to sew and reap and plant and fill my warehouses with fruit so that I will lack nothing." Such were his intentions, but that night he died. Whoever has ears, let him hear. (saying #63)

PARABLE OF THE INVITED GUEST

This being human is a guest house. Every morning is a new arrival. A joy, a depression, a meanness, some momentary awareness comes as an unexpected visitor...Welcome and entertain them all. Treat each guest honorably. The dark thought, the shame, the malice, meet them at the door laughing, and invite them in. Be grateful for whoever comes, because each has been sent as a guide from beyond.
—Rumi

The Parable

Now he told a parable to those who were invited, when he noticed how they chose the places of honor, saying to them, "When you are invited by someone to a wedding feast, do not sit down in a place of honor, lest someone more distinguished than you be invited by him, and he who invited you both will come and say to you, 'Give your place to this person,' and then you will begin with shame to take the lowest place. But when you are invited, go and sit in the lowest place, so that when your host comes he may say to you, 'Friend, move up higher.' Then you will be honored in the presence of all who sit at table with you. For everyone who exalts himself will be humbled, and he who humbles himself will be exalted."

He said also to the man who had invited him, "When you give a dinner or a banquet, do not invite your friends or your brothers or your relatives or rich neighbors, lest they also invite you in return and you be repaid. But when you give a feast, invite the poor, the crippled, the lame, the blind, and you will be blessed, because they cannot repay you. For you will be repaid at the resurrection of the just." Luke 14:7-14

The Hidden Meaning

Humility

Christ does not want us to boast or elevate ourselves. We should not seek praise or esteem. Let these come to us uninvited. It is far better to be showered with praise than to demand it.

Whoever humbles himself like this child is the greatest in the kingdom of heaven. Matt 18:4

Honoring self

We honor self, not by showing off, demanding respect and honor from others, but rather by how we treat ourselves. By caring for our bodies, minds, emotions and spirit we honor our self. We are important because we are unique expressions of the cosmic. So is everyone else. If we toot our own horn, we might be disappointed for there will aways be someone better than we are at some function or activity. It is best to leave the honoring to someone else. Even then, we should be humbled that we are being recognized.

We are invited to a wedding feast

Our birth on earth is an invitation to a wedding feast. It is easy to get used to earth's beauty and richness and take it for granted and ignore it. It takes open eyes, attentive ears and sensitive hearts to fully appreciate our beautiful and diverse planet. Earth has everything we could ever want to experience, enjoy, and be awed by. It is a matter of attitude. Christ is reminding us again and again to celebrate our lives as if we are at a wedding. We should "dress" appropriately for the occasion —cheerful expression, grateful hearts and humility for having been an invited guest.

Exalting/humbling self

When Christ says: "For everyone who exalts himself will be humbled, and he who humbles himself will be exalted", He wants our actions, behavior and lifestyle to speak for themselves. If we are worthy of honoring, then we will be honored and if we are not honored, so what. We know who we are and we are comfortable within our skin. Our self-esteem does not depend on how we are treated by others. It depends on how we view and treat ourselves.

There is much wisdom in what Christ advocates. It is far better to be honored without seeking it than to be disappointed by seeking honor and not getting it.

When we give a dinner banquet

Inviting people to a dinner party is honoring them. Christ advocates for helping those who cannot help themselves. People who are well off do not need our service. It is pointless to "invite them to our wedding". Who we need to "invite to our wedding" are those who are in need of assistance.

Christ is asking us to honor those we extend a helping hand to as honored guests and not as someone beneath us.

Personalizing the Parable

Life can be a roller coaster with many ups and downs. Most of us, at one time or another, will need the assistance of another. I certainly did. I have experienced both types of assistance. I have known those who give so they are recognized and praised and I have known those who give anonymously, not letting the left hand know what the right hand is doing. More importantly, some give in the spirit of superiority dishonoring the receiver as an inferior. The best givers are those who give gladly, anonymously and honor the receiver. These charitable individuals feel honored to have had the opportunity to be of assistance. No reward or recognition is required.

Why the Parable?

This parable is about humility. The word humility is derived from Latin "humilis" meaning "low." We know what happens to plants that lay low when a storm comes. They survive. Christ, in this parable is advising us to stay low, not be proud. And what do we have that we can be proud of?

- Is it our accomplishments?
- Perhaps it is our intelligence.
- Maybe we can be proud of our skills and abilities.
- What about our possessions?

Our accomplishments are not solely due to our efforts. We stand on the shoulders of all those who preceded us. Our knowledge is cumulative. We learn from each other. We build on what others have learned. We benefit from each other's discovery. We learn from our teachers who learned from their teachers. We read books and absorb the experiences of the authors. Whatever we accomplish is a mere link in the ever-growing chain of the accomplishments of humanity.

Our intelligence is a mere gift of our brain and genetic makeup. Obviously, we have a role to play in cultivating our minds, but we still stand on the shoulders of others. Rarely do we create our own brand-new breakthroughs. Even when we do, it is the gift of inspiration.

Our skills and abilities are gifts as well. I never forget the day when I woke up in the middle of the night to use the bathroom. Suddenly, something went wrong in my lower back. I collapsed to the floor as if an electrical switch got turned off. I was unable to move. Crawling an inch at a time to make it to the bathroom, left an indelible mark in my consciousness as to what humility entails. How can we be proud of our skills and abilities when it is the miraculous workings of the body that enable us to do all that we do? How can we take the credit? Our problem is that while we have something, we rarely appreciate its value until we lose it. Take walking for instance. While we can walk, we take walking for granted. Once we lose our ability to walk, then we realize the full value of walking.

Our possessions are not something we should be proud of. They are temporary and are meant to be enjoyed while they last. Possessions get old, damaged and they are replaced.

So, what else can we be proud of? Nothing. Hence, humility is the best attitude to have. It is wise to follow Christ's advice. Staying humble is the best course to follow.

PARABLE OF THE LOST COIN

It is good to have money and the things that money can buy, but it's good too, to check up once in a while and make sure you haven't lost the things money can't buy. —George Horace Lorimer

The Parable

"Or what woman, having ten silver coins, if she loses one coin, does not light a lamp and sweep the house and seek diligently until she finds it? And when she has found it, she calls together her friends and neighbors, saying, 'Rejoice with me, for I have found the coin that I had lost.' Just so, I tell you, there is joy before the angels of God over one sinner who repents." Luke 15:8-10

The Hidden Meaning

Ten silver coins

Coins are symbolic of monetary value. The coins are valuable because they are silver. As mentioned earlier, ten is the number for the cosmos. It symbolizes all manifestations. Ten contains all the digits from zero to nine. Hence, it contains all. When we have all ten, we feel complete, fulfilled and satisfied. When we lose one, we feel the opposite—incomplete, unfulfilled and dissatisfied.

Losing one coin

This is one of the few instances where Christ weaves a parable around a woman. The implication is that women usually do not have much wealth on their own. Hence, losing one silver coin is very relevant for this lady. The woman, having lost one of her 10 silver coins, no longer feels complete. Something important is missing. She will not be satisfied until she finds it.

Christ in this parable is letting us know that we are the lost silver coin and that we are very valuable. Our master will not be satisfied until we change course and head back home. The master within will not rest until we are found.

Lighting a lamp

We cannot search for what is lost while in the dark. We must light a lamp. We must have a source of light. The light we need is spiritual light. It is within us as knowledge, wisdom and understanding. We ignite this light when we are earnest in our search, eager to seek and anxious to find and feel fulfilled.

Sweeping the house

We sweep the house to get rid of dirt, junk and debris. Our house is our life. It is our body, our emotions and our mind. Our mind houses our habits, attitudes, expectations and beliefs. These must be examined, tossing out the unwanted, superfluous, superstition and fear-based. We should sweep our house on a regular basis. Our house must be immaculately clean containing only what we deem important.

Seeking diligently

To find, our seeking must be diligent, our knocking loud and persistent and our asking must be heartfelt. The answer will come at the appropriate moment when we least expect it. The lost item will be found if we search in earnest.

Finding the coin

Once we ask, knock and seek, we must trust and let go. The lamp within will guide us. Our eyes will open and we will see. Our ears will clear and we will hear and our hearts will soften and we will feel alive. We will find our way back to our source, the Kingdom of God within. We are the lost coin searching to know our true self.

Rejoicing and celebrating

Finding, we will rejoice and celebrate. We will *"call together our friends and neighbors, saying, 'Rejoice with me, for I have found the coin that I had lost."*

Finding our path, our entire body will tingle with joy. We will be at peace and satisfied. Our lives will convert to a wedding feast where we are the honored guests.

Personalizing the Parable

We are in the world and like the Prodigal son, we have lost our way. The distractions of the world are numerous. We set out seeking pleasure, entertainment and amusement. We found these and we immersed ourselves in them wallowing in forgetfulness. After a while, we realized that there is no satisfaction in what we are doing. The pleasures are temporary, the entertainment short-lived and the amusement is at our expense. We wake up. "What am I doing living like this?" We realize how wasteful and meaningless our lives have been. We conclude that there must be something better, something more enduring that we could pursue. We seek that which gives value and meaning to our lives. There is something missing in our lives and we need to know what it is. We cry out in anguish. We ask, we seek and we knock. Our sincerity and persistence are rewarded. Finding the coin is finding ourselves.

Why the Parable?

With this parable Christ is imprinting on us that we are the lost silver coin and that we are individually valuable. Like the shepherd who left the 99 sheep to search for the one missing sheep, the "woman" deemed it important to look for the one lost coin. She lit the lamp, swept the house and she sought diligently. We are the shepherd, the woman and the lost coin. We need to light the lamp of reason, sweep the junk in our lives aside and fearlessly seek answers that satisfy our souls. We have a guide within that will show us the way. We will find the truth and the truth will set us free. We will feel liberated. Finding ourselves will be a rebirth into spirituality.

What is sin?

> *"there is joy before the angels of God over one sinner who repents."*

Sin is defined as *"an action, thought, or feeling that goes against a divine law or standard. Different cultures have their own interpretations of sin."* We have been told that we have all sinned and that there isn't a single person without sin. We are told that because of the original sin, we are all born in sin. If sin is anything against a divine law or standard, then how can anyone sin? A divine law is issued from divinity—God. Under the Old system, there were hundreds or even a thousand laws issued that we were expected to comply with. Breaking any of them would constitute sin, an infringement against a divine dictate. Fortunately, we are no longer under the Law; we are in Grace. Christ gave us one and only one commandment that we should love with all of our hearts—love God, our neighbor and ourselves. In other words, the only sin we can commit is not to love when we can.

There is one more sin that I am aware of and that is **ignoring our conscience**. Acting contrary to the dictates of our conscience is referred to as "sinning against the Holy Spirit." This is a serious offence indeed.

What is repentance?

In general terms, living in sin implies being lost—on the path that leads nowhere. Repenting is realizing that we are lost, on the wrong path and making an about face. It is like finding the lost coin. Instantly, what we value and deem important changes. We reverse course and head to our Father who is waiting for us with open arms. We will be welcomed home where we belong. Repenting is making amends for all the harm we might have caused. It is discovering the Kingdom within and rejoicing.

PARABLE OF THE RICH MAN AND LAZARUS

Wealth and poverty do not lie in a man's estate, but in men's souls. —Antisthenes

The Parable

"There was a rich man who was clothed in purple and fine linen and who feasted sumptuously every day. And at his gate was laid a poor man named Lazarus, covered with sores, who desired to be fed with what fell from the rich man's table. Moreover, even the dogs came and licked his sores. The poor man died and was carried by the angels to Abraham's side. The rich man also died and was buried, and in Hades, being in torment, he lifted up his eyes and saw Abraham far off and Lazarus at his side. And he called out, 'Father Abraham, have mercy on me, and send Lazarus to dip the end of his finger in water and cool my tongue, for I am in anguish in this flame.' But Abraham said, 'Child, remember that you in your lifetime received your good things, and Lazarus in like manner bad things; but now he is comforted here, and you are in anguish. And besides all this, between us and you a great chasm has been fixed, in order that those who would pass from here to you may not be able, and none may cross from there to us.' And he said, 'Then I beg you, father, to send him to my father's house—for I have five brothers—so that he may warn them, lest they also come into this place of torment.' But Abraham said, 'They have

Moses and the Prophets; let them hear them.' And he said, 'No, father Abraham, but if someone goes to them from the dead, they will repent.' He said to him, 'If they do not hear Moses and the Prophets, neither will they be convinced if someone should rise from the dead.'" Luke 16:19-31

The Hidden Meaning

Rich man

There are many instances where Christ gives the impression that being rich is a negative quality. It is not. When He says, *"it is harder for a rich man to go to heaven than a rope to go through the eye of a needle"*, He has the greedy rich in mind. There are two types of wealthy people. The first type are those who use their wealth to control others, influence public opinions, further their own agenda, spread falsehoods and distort facts. This type of the rich are greedy, unscrupulous and obsessed with wealth and power. They are without conscience. There is a second type of wealthy people who endeavor to do good. They build museums, libraries, hospitals, give out scholarships, pay for vaccinations, donate works of art and do charitable work. I can assume that Christ does not have these people in mind when He condemns the wealthy. Mary Magdalene was a wealthy woman. She used her wealth to support Christ and His disciples. The rich man in the above parable was only into himself, adorning himself in purple and fine linen and who dined sumptuously every day without sharing anything with the needy, not even his leftovers.

Clothed in purple and fine linen

Purple is the color of royalty. Silk and fine linen are of exceptional quality. This rich man spared nothing for his physical comfort. His only focus was luxury, comfort and personal pleasure. According to Christ, the only wealth that matters is spiritual wealth.

Feasted sumptuously daily

Feasting sumptuously daily is taking care of the physical body only. While the physical body is getting more than it needs, the spiritual body is being neglected.

> "But he answered, "It is written, "'Man shall not live by bread alone, but by every word that comes from the mouth of God.'" Matt 4:4

We need spiritual food—contemplation, prayer, meditation and inspirational reading in addition to our physical nourishment.

Lazarus, poor and covered in sores

Lazarus was poor materially and he had many problems (covered in sores), yet, he had a gentle soul, a kind and humble spirit. He was a good person.

> "Blessed are the poor in spirit, for theirs is the kingdom of heaven." Matt 5:3

Desired to be fed with leftovers

Lazarus did not ask for much, just some leftovers. He was humble. He did not require much to be satisfied.

Dogs licked his sores

This is to show that even though the rich human did not have any compassion, the dogs did. They acted with care and compassion. The dogs, in this parable, set an example for us to emulate.

Lazarus was in heaven, the rich man was in hell

Christ is telling us that the reward for humility and goodness is "heaven "while that for selfishness and evil is "hell." We do not know what exactly Christ meant by these terms. They could not have been literal, physical places since on many occasions, He emphasized that His Kingdom is not physical. It is spiritual. Heaven and hell must be spiritual states of being.

Lazarus was in Abraham's bosom

Being in someone's bosom is being in their consciousness, awareness and protection. Obviously, this is metaphorical. Imagine all the people in heaven literally being in Abraham's bosom.

I am in anguish in this flame

The rich man in hell feels anguish, not heat. He is not burning. He is spiritually tormented with anguish. This is exactly how one with regrets would feel after death.

A chasm exists between heaven and hell

We know heaven and hell are allegorical because the rich man, while in hell, can see into heaven. He sees Lazarus in the bosom of Abraham. He can even converse with those in heaven. This would be impossible if these were physical locations separated by a chasm. This can happen only if heaven and hell are allegorical.

The chasm that exists between heaven and earth is spiritual and is only in consciousness.

Moses and the prophets

Christ is telling us that there have been several teachers and spiritual leaders who appeared on earth and taught us spiritual truths. If we had eyes to see and ears to hear, we would have understood and changed course. Enough has already been revealed to us. More would not make any difference. Because Christ was addressing Jews, He mentioned people they are familiar with such as Moses and the prophets.

Conviction and the need for proof

The rich man wanted his five brothers to have proof of the afterlife.

What constitutes proof?

What would it take to convince us?

The rich man wanted Lazarus, a dead man, to go back to earth and warn his siblings. Christ said that even if Lazarus did go back, no one would believe him. He knew what He is talking about for He experienced it himself. He raised Lazarus from the grave. Did the Judeans believe in Him? No. They not only sought to kill Him, but sought to kill Lazarus as well to blot out the proof from their midst.

The Plot to Kill Lazarus

> When the large crowd of the Jews learned that Jesus was there, they came, not only on account of him but also to see Lazarus, whom he had raised from the dead. So the chief priests made plans to put Lazarus to death as well, because on account of him many of the Jews were going away and believing in Jesus. John 12:9-11

Personalizing the Parable

Lazarus wanted only the leftovers from the rich man's table. In other words, Christ is letting us know that we only need to share what we have in excess.

In the material sense, when we give something, we lose it. We no longer have it. Yet, the spiritual laws demonstrate that when we give a little, in the spirit of Christ—love and compassion, we gain much more in return. When we enrich someone else's life, we become enriched several times over.

If we want to act with compassion and make a difference in

someone's life, here and now is where we can do it. We cannot do it after we die. Here is the arena of action. This is where we can make a difference. This is where we can take advantage of our opportunities and make a positive contribution.

Why the Parable?

- Life on Earth is temporary. Soon we will die. Only the inner self survives death. The body and the ego disintegrate and are no more. The inner self can survive only if it is spiritualized. In other words, the more spiritual we are, the more awake and alive we are.

- We can only do good while we are alive and have an opportunity to act.

- We are in the spirit after we die. It is there that we review our lives. This is why the rich man can see Lazarus mentally. He was reliving his main actions and their consequences. This is his judgment hall. He feels anguish at his regrettable actions. He must learn from his mistakes and resolve to do better. He also can feel satisfaction from his well-thought actions. Our anguishes and our satisfactions are the hell and heaven that we experience after we die.

- Wealth is a resource. If ill managed, it enslaves, blinds and distracts us. If well managed, it can work wonders in our life and in the lives of others.

- If we are wealthy, all we need to give away and share is the excess that we do not need (our leftovers).

PARABLE OF THE PERSISTENT WIDOW

Success is almost totally dependent upon drive and persistence. The extra energy required to make another effort or try another approach is the secret of winning.
—Denis Waitley

The Parable

And he told them a parable to the effect that they ought always to pray and not lose heart. He said, "In a certain city there was a judge who neither feared God nor respected man. And there was a widow in that city who kept coming to him and saying, 'Give me justice against my adversary.' For a while he refused, but afterward he said to himself, 'Though I neither fear God nor respect man, yet because this widow keeps bothering me, I will give her justice, so that she will not beat me down by her continual coming.'" And the Lord said, "Hear what the unrighteous judge says. And will not God give justice to his elect, who cry to him day and night? Will he delay long over them? I tell you, he will give justice to them speedily. Nevertheless, when the Son of Man comes, will he find faith on earth?" Luke 18:1-8

The Hidden Meaning

Why a widow?

The widow is a woman, perhaps old, who has lost her husband. She is a metaphor for someone who is without a protector or means to defend her case. She is insignificant as far as material position and power are concerned. Yet, she has an internal strength that compensates for all that she lacks. She is doggedly persistent.

Who is the judge?

A judge who neither feared God nor respected man is someone very difficult to sway one way or another. This judge is fearless, dispassionate and steady as a rock. His heart is unyielding. Yet, persistence melts the hardest of hearts.

Pray and don't lose heart

In times of difficulty and when we are challenged to our limit, Christ is advising us to pray and not lose heart. Prayer, according to Christ, is in two phases: First, we enter our "closet", a private place where we meditate and commune with the God within us, our Inner Spiritual Self. Next, we ask passionately, knock loudly and seek earnestly. We express gratitude and we let go. We live our normal lives until suddenly we hear the Voice Within providing us with an answer, or guiding us to a solution. Once we know what we need to do, we do not hesitate. We act fearlessly.

Persistence

We persist when we know we are right, are wholeheartedly convinced and we strongly believe in our cause. Persistence is not stubbornness. It is tenacity in the face of adversity. It is determination in the face of obstacles. It is resolve when others doubt us. Persistence is not giving up until we have our answer.

Justice

The widow was seeking justice. But can we ever have true justice? In most cases, there can never be any justice. What if a drunkard kills a loved one? In this case, the only possible justice is if the killer experiences the consequence for his or her actions. This can only happen through karma via reincarnation. Justice in most cases is compensation and an inner satisfaction that something was done to alleviate the injustice. In the widow's case, all she wanted was fairness, impartiality and compensation.

Who are God's elect?

In the "Old" age, God's elect were those who God had chosen for salvation. This is not true in the "New" age of Grace, the age of Christ. If God chooses who will be saved, then there is not much we can do. In the Old days, Yahweh chose his people and they came to be known as "The Chosen, or The Elect." This ended with John the Baptist. A New era began with Christ. There are no longer any pre-selected chosen people. The *"elect and the chosen"* are now the ones who do the choosing themselves. Our salvation now is in our own hands. If we believe and act in the spirit of Christ, then we become God's elect and we determine our fate.

What is faith?

> *"When the Son of Man comes, will he find faith on earth?"*

Christ often referred to his contemporaries as *"people with little or no faith."* He also, on several occasions, told people that their faith healed them.

> *Jesus turned, and seeing her he said, "Take heart, daughter; your faith has made you well." And instantly the woman was made well. Matt 9:22*

Christ expects us to have faith, but what is faith? According to Christ, our faith has to be a conviction so strong that "it can move mountains".

> *Truly, I say to you, whoever says to this mountain, 'Be taken up and thrown into the sea,' and does not doubt in his heart, but believes that what he says will come to pass, it will be done for him. Mark 11:23*

And what are mountains? They are the difficulties and the challenges we face during the course of living. At times, these appear to be insurmountable. However, through faith, they can be converted into opportunities, especially for spiritual growth.

And how do we develop such faith? By becoming pure, innocent, inquisitive and trusting in ourselves and the Kingdom within like little children. This faith cannot be vaporous. It must be based on solid ground so that no wind, storm or hurricane can blow it away. The solid foundation of faith is knowledge based on experience, specifically, knowing who we are, loving ourselves and following the dictates of our conscience when expressing ourselves.

Personalizing the Parable

Not many of us are wealthy, powerful or with important connections. What we lack externally, we can develop and strengthen internally. These are confidence, fearlessness, conviction, persistence, faith and belief in ourself and the God within. These are permanent qualities and are much more important to have than the fickle external appearances of power through position of authority and material wealth.

Why the Parable?

- Christ wants us to cultivate perseverance, tenacity,

determination, doggedness and resolve.
- We need to cultivate faith based on knowledge and personal experience.
- We control our own fate. We determine our future based on the decisions we make and the actions we take.
- We should never give up or lose heart.
- Spiritual wealth is more valuable than material wealth.
- We can move mountains through knowledge, faith and confidence in our self.
- Persistence can soften the hardest of hearts; it can drill through the toughest resistance.

PARABLE OF THE PHARISEE AND THE TAX COLLECTOR

Be a light unto others, not boastful of self. —Edgar Cayce

The Parable

He also told this parable to some who trusted in themselves that they were righteous, and treated others with contempt: "Two men went up into the temple to pray, one a Pharisee and the other a tax collector. The Pharisee, standing by himself, prayed thus: 'God, I thank you that I am not like other men, extortioners, unjust, adulterers, or even like this tax collector. I fast twice a week; I give tithes of all that I get.' But the tax collector, standing far off, would not even lift up his eyes to heaven, but beat his breast, saying, 'God, be merciful to me, a sinner!' I tell you, this man went down to his house justified, rather than the other. For everyone who exalts himself will be humbled, but the one who humbles himself will be exalted." Luke 18:9-14

The Hidden Meaning

Who is the Pharisee?

The pharisee represents people in power, the clergy, the politicians, the wealthy and the well-connected. St. Paul lived as a Pharisee before his conversion. He persecuted early followers of Jesus all the way to Damascus. The "Pharisees" are those who do good just to be noticed. They are the ones who sit at positions of honor during festivities. They are full of themselves, proud and self-righteous. They believe that they are privileged and are above ordinary people.

Who is the Tax Collector?

> "In Jesus' time, there was nobody more hated than tax collectors (also known as publicans). Unlike the collectors of today, publicans were considered traitors. They cheated, stole, and extorted money from people to line their pockets and the treasury of a foreign occupier." The Internet

In other words, the tax collector represents the lowest of the lowly. In this case, they are the common, ordinary people, the dejected and the despised.

Boasting and bragging

> "Some who trusted in themselves that they were righteous, and treated others with contempt".

These are the ones who believe they are right and everyone else is wrong. These people are into impressing others of their importance. Often, those in power believe they are right and above everyone else because of their wealth, position and status.

The Pharisee knew he was righteous. He bragged that he was not like the tax collector. He looked with contempt at the tax collector. He believed he deserved mercy because he fasted and tithed.

In modern times we still have those who behave like the Pharisee in how they treat others who are unlike themselves.

Humility

The tax collector beat his chest to demonstrate his sorrow. He cried out to God for mercy because he knew he was a sinner who desperately needed mercy and forgiveness.

Instead of considering himself righteous, the tax collector pleaded to God for mercy. He knew he was a sinner. He did not pretend that he was righteous. He bared his heart and soul and asked for mercy and forgiveness.

Justified

Other words for justified are: one is right, vindicated, acceptable and correct. In other words, the tax collector's prayers were accepted because he knew he was sinful and admitted it. The Pharisee bragged about how good he was. He was righteous and he beat his own drum. He advertised and boasted about his righteousness. His prayers fell on deaf ears.

Lifting up the eyes/lowering the eyes

It is customary to lower the eyes while addressing a superior out of respect. The tax collector would not look at heaven while praying. He chose a far off location to pray. He lowered his eyes and he beat his chest in admission of his shortfalls. Unlike the Pharisee, he did not recount any of his virtues.

The way of Christ

"God, I thank you that I am not like other men, extortioners, unjust, adulterers, or even like this tax collector. I fast twice a week; I give tithes of all that I get."
–The Pharisee

"Standing far off, would not even lift up his eyes to heaven, but beat his breast, saying, 'God, be merciful to me, a sinner!" –the tax collector

"For everyone who exalts himself will be humbled, but the one who humbles himself will be exalted." –Christ

Christ taught us that he who wants to be the greatest must serve the most. It is a new era where the first will be last and the last will be first. It is an era of humility, service, sacrifice and love. In this new philosophy, status counts for naught. It is what is in the heart that matters most.

Personalizing the Parable

Having the Kingdom of God within, we do not need to go anywhere to pray. We can do it where we are, in silence, in reverence and from the heart. We do not even need to pray. Our prayer radiates as the essence of who we are. In fact, we are always praying.

We do not need to be awed by authority figures either. It is not their rank and status that matters. It is their intentions and the actions they render.

Why the Parable?

- We need to be sincere and practice humility.
- What matters is purity of heart, not social standing or appearance.
- "Blessed are the meek, for they shall inherit the earth." Matt 5:5
- God is not fooled by outer displays of piety. God can see and read hearts.
- If we exalt ourselves, there is nowhere to go but down.
- If we humble ourselves, there is nowhere to go but up.
- To follow Christ, we need to adopt a new attitude—humility and meekness.

In several parables Christ emphasizes the dawn of a new age. In this age, it is not the proud or the prominent who are the virtuous. Rather, it is the humble and the meek for they shall inherit the Earth. *"Extortioners, unjust, adulterers, or even like this tax collector"*, are closer to being accepted by God if they humble themselves and confess their shortcomings than those who exalt themselves, are proud or publicly exhibit their piety. Abiding by the laws no longer guarantees redemption. Sincerity, purity of heart, admission of guilt and the resolve to do better are the way to redemption.

Even fasting and tithing are useless unless they are carried out humbly and sincerely. Through this parable, Christ wants us to know the importance of praying with the right attitude. This parable is aimed at the Pharisees and people like them who think they are righteous and look down on others.

The Parable from Other Sources

The Parable of the Two Sons (Matthew)

> *"What do you think? A man had two sons. And he went to the first and said, 'Son, go and work in the vineyard today.' And he answered, 'I will not,' but afterward he changed his mind and went. And he went to the other son and said the same. And he answered, 'I go, sir,' but did not go. Which of the two did the will of his father?" They said, "The first." Jesus said to them, "Truly, I say to you, the tax collectors and the prostitutes go into the kingdom of God before you. For John came to you in the way of righteousness, and you did not believe him, but the tax collectors and the prostitutes believed him. And even when you saw it, you did not afterward change your minds and believe him. Matt 21:28-32*

It is not what we say or believe that matters. It is what we actually do. Actions speak louder than any words.

THE LIFE OF JESUS CHRIST AS A PARABLE

I am encouraged as I look at some of those who have listened to their "different drum": Einstein was hopeless at school math and commented wryly on his inadequacy in human relations. Winston Churchill was an abysmal failure in his early school years. Byron, that revolutionary student, had to compensate for a club foot; Demosthenes for a stutter; and Homer was blind. Socrates couldn't manage his wife, and infuriated his countrymen. And what about Jesus, if we need an ultimate example of failure with one's peers? Or an ultimate example of love? —Madeleine L'Engle

Many consider the life of Jesus Christ as a historic event that took place some 2000 years ago. That is one way to look at it. However, the history of early Christianity is not something concrete for scarcely any historic evidence exists about the actual life of Jeus Christ. The gospels could not have been written by the Apostles or any eye-witnesses. There were hundreds of books written about Christ in the early years. There were numerous Christian sects that differed vastly in their interpretation of what Christ's message was. The vast majority of these books were considered heretical and were banned, burned or destroyed.

The synoptic gospels have many contradictions. This is because the books were hand-copied, not from originals, but from other hand copies. If anyone needed a copy of a manuscript, it had to be copied manually. We must keep in mind that there were no printing presses or copying machines in those days. According to professor Bart Ehrman, all the books we have are copies of copies which are copies of other copies until the invention of the printing press in 1440 A.D. It was not until 1454 A.D., however, that Gutenberg made his printing press available for commercial use. The earliest New Testament Gospel that we have is that of Mark which is from around 350 A.D. which was originally handwritten around the year 70 A.D. There are no original copies of any of the manuscripts of the New Testament.

Instead of looking for the historical Jesus and the historical writings about Jesus, it is far better to look at Christ and His message from the spiritual point of view. We can find the spiritual teachings of Christ in His parables. The hidden messages buried within these parables are what we need to uncover. These are the light that will guide our footsteps on the path to not only an ethical and moral life, but also to spirituality and the discovery of the divine within.

Christ showed us the way to the abundant life through love and service. In fact, this is the secret to business success as well. Loving customers and giving them the best service possible will ensure the success of that business. Christ had a higher purpose, though. He wanted to tell us how to tend the spark within so it will become a flame. He could not do that outright because, as He put it:

> *Therefore speak I to them in parables: because they seeing see not; and hearing they hear not, neither do they understand. Matt 13:13*

The Life of Jesus Christ

The life of Christ is a prototype of the possible life. We go through similar stages that Christ went through. He came to show us the way by living and by being the way. He came to demonstrate the purpose of life by the mission of His life. He wanted us to know that we are much more than we appear to be—a physical body. He told us that all that He did we can do as well. He told us who He was—a child of God so that we know who we are—children of God. He suffered and was persecuted to let us know that this can and will happen to us as well. He even showed us how to respond to those who persecute us—with patience, understanding, sympathy and compassion.

Nativity and Visitation

Jesus was born in Bethlehem. "Beth" means house and "Lehem" means bread. Bethlehem is the house of bread. This is metaphoric since Christ is the "house of bread." He is the bread of life.

> *And Jesus said unto them, I am the bread of life: he that cometh to me shall never hunger; and he that believeth on me shall never thirst. John 6:35*
>
> *I am the living bread which came down from heaven: if any man eat of this bread, he shall live for ever: and the bread that I will give is my flesh, which I will give for the life of the world. John 6:51*

This bread, however, is not physical bread. It is His teachings, the spiritual messages which He imparted to His disciples.

> *But he answered, "It is written, "'Man shall not live by bread alone, but by every word that comes from the mouth of God.'" Matt 4:4*

We do not know where exactly Jesus was born whether it was a cave, a manger or a stable. These are symbols for humility. When He was born, the shepherds rejoiced in the fields. So it is with the vast majority of people. Most of us are born in humble places and there is rejoicing for our birth, specifically by our parents, family and relatives.

Three wise men, or magi, came to visit the Christ child bearing gifts. This, too is symbolic. For the magi to come on camelback all the way from Persia or Chaldea would have taken an enormous amount of time. Christ was in the manger perhaps a day or two. We know this is symbolic because of the gifts they brought to the child.

- Gold
- Frankincense
- Myrrh

And when they were come into the house, they saw the young child with Mary his mother, and fell down, and worshipped him: and when they had opened their treasures, they presented unto him gifts; gold, and frankincense, and myrrh. Matt 2:11

Gold is the royal metal, valuable and desirable. Gold is a metaphor for the Alchemical transmutation we must accomplish converting tin into gold. In other words, this is the purpose of life—the transformation of our vices into virtues, our weaknesses into strengths and our challenges into opportunities. If we do, we grow and become enlightened.

Frankincense is symbolic of purity and virtue. This is the incense we burn in our churches to purify the air and to sanctify the place of worship. In other words, we transmute our base qualities into noble ones by living a virtuous life with a pure heart and a noble mind.

Myrrh is symbolic of suffering and death. It was presented to Christ both at birth and at death. This is a reminder that all those who are born, will suffer and eventually die.

And they gave him to drink wine mingled with myrrh: but he received it not. Mark 15:23

We, too are presented with gifts when we are born. These gifts are innate talents, skills and abilities. These must be developed and put to good use. We are expected to use these gifts effectively not only to transform our lives, but to enhance the quality of life of others as well. During the course of living, we are presented with many opportunities. If we take advantage of these, we set ourselves on an accelerated path to spiritual development. We are entrusted with our gifts of talents, skills and abilities. We are expected to, at least, double their value by the end of our lives. This is the purpose of our lives.

Escape to Egypt

King Herod wanted to kill Jesus to prevent Him from becoming King. Knowing this, the family escaped to Egypt. King Herod ordered the killing of all children two years of age and younger. It is very difficult to imagine something like this could be historic. This is as bad as the Lord in the Old Testament ordering the murder of the first born of the Egyptians. Jesus with His mother and father remained in Egypt until Herod passed away and there was no longer a threat on the life of Jesus.

> *And was there until the death of Herod: saying, Out of Egypt have I called my son. Matt 2:15*

This "***out of Egypt have I called my son***" is not in reference to Jesus. It refers to Israel. (See Appendix A). Whenever we read in the gospels that something happened "*that it might be fulfilled which was spoken of the Lord by the prophet,*" we know that this is an addition specifically inserted into the gospels to prove that Jesus was the expected Messiah as prophesized in the Old Testament. This is done to attract Jews into Christianity. There are no prophesies in the Old Testament about the future birth of Jesus. These additions are for the sake of linking the New with the Old to convince the Jews and the pagans that Christianity was not a new religion. (according to Dr. Bart Ehrman).

From Egypt the family returned to Nazareth. We do not hear from Jesus again until He was twelve years old and was in the temple astonishing the elders with his knowledge.

Baptism

When Jesus was 30 years old, He was baptized by John the Baptist. The heavens opened and the Holy Spirit descended on Him in the form of a dove and a voice was heard from the heavens proclaiming: " . . . *This is my beloved Son, in whom I am well pleased." Matt 3:17* This is when Jesus became the Christ and His mission began. Hearing the voice, Jesus knew who He was and He was ready. He went to the wilderness for 40 days and 40 nights where He was tempted by the Devil. He triumphed. He started calling His disciples, one or two at a time until He had 12.

His Mission

His mission was to live an exemplary life showing us the way to the abundant life. He lived to emphasize compassion, being non-judgmental, loving and serving. Instead of fearing God, He showed us how to love God as our heavenly Father. His public teachings were distilled in His Sermon on the Mount. He wanted to steer us away from the barbaric old way and have us embrace the gentle new way. He could not teach this openly for fear of an early demise. Instead, He encapsulated these teachings into the parables.

Another reason He taught people via parables was because they could not understand and appreciate what He wanted to tell them. The people had eyes, but they could not see. They had ears, but they could not hear and understand. They had hearts, but they could not feel compassion. He taught openly and in detail to His disciples and close associates explaining the mysteries of the Kingdom of Heaven which are buried deep within each individual.

Even though He healed the sick, cast out evil spirits from the possessed and raised the dead back to life, He had few believers. The establishment, meanwhile, sought to kill Him.

He was transfigured while on a mountaintop. He began to shine and became "white as the light." Moses and Elijiah appeared next to Him and a voice proclaimed, once more, that He was the beloved Son of God.

> *He was still speaking when, behold, a bright cloud overshadowed them, and a voice from the cloud said, "This is my beloved Son, with whom I am well pleased; listen to him."* Matt 17:5

Disciples

Christ called to himself 12 disciples to be His intimate companions. The 12 disciples represent the road to mastery. This is allegorical signifying that in order to gain mastery and be Christlike, we must perfect 12 disciplines—6 virtues that we must cultivate and 6 vices that we must shun or eradicate. For example, Peter represented virtue and faith while Judas represented the vice of greed, treachery and distrust. Judas was Christ's Achilles Heel. He was the weak link that ended up being the cause of His death by crucifixion.

In order to gain mastery, we too must decide on 6 virtues that we must cultivate and 6 vices that we must overcome and eradicate. We, too, will have a "Judas" in our lives. This is going to be our Achilles Heel, a vice or a weakness, such as an accident, a disease or an infirmity that will cause our eventual death.

Faith

Christ wanted us to have faith. On one occasion His disciples could not heal an epileptic and when they asked Christ for the reason, He told them that they lacked the necessary faith. On several occasions Christ told those He healed that it was their faith that healed them.

What is faith?

Faith is a belief involving both the heart and the mind resulting in action. Faith is not blind, far from it. It is not accepting beliefs without questioning. True faith is belief in ourselves, in our knowledge and in our abilities. Faith based on knowledge and conviction stemming from personal experience is unshakable. Christ wanted us to question even the prophets.

> *And he said to them, "O foolish ones, and slow of heart to believe all that the prophets have spoken! Luke 24:25*

When Peter, while walking on water, began to doubt himself, he began to sink.

> *He said, "Come." So Peter got out of the boat and walked on the water and came to Jesus. But when he saw the wind, he was afraid, and beginning to sink he cried out, "Lord, save me." Jesus immediately reached out his hand and took hold of him, saying to him, "O you of little faith, why did you doubt?" Matt 14:29-31*

> *He said to them, "Because of your little faith. For truly, I say to you, if you have faith like a grain of mustard seed, you will say to this mountain, 'Move from here to there,' and it will move, and nothing will be impossible for you." Matt 17:20*

The faith Christ wants us to have is "as a grain of mustard seed." This does not mean small. The mustard seed is what the Kingdom of Heaven is like and it is within us. In other words, when we discover the Kingdom of God within, it will be in the form and size of a mustard seed. Initially, our faith will be miniscule, like a seed. Like a seedling, it must be nurtured and allowed to grow into a magnificent tree. Then, our faith will be strong enough to move any mountain, the mountain being a challenge, or an obstacle in our way.

Eschatology

Christ did not come to proclaim the imminent end of the world. It is obvious that He was referring to something that would take place in His lifetime.

> *"Repent, for the kingdom of heaven is at hand." Matt 3:2*

Christ's was referring to the end of the **Old:** old covenant, old mentality of violence, aggression and the confiscation of other people's property. At the same time, He was proclaiming the birth of the **New**: a new covenant of the heart, a covenant of love, service, compassion, forgiveness and acceptance.

Does the Old way lead to God? Yes, but it is the long and tortuous way. Like everything else in life, there are two ways to get someplace. We can go straight to our objective or we can go the opposite direction going around the entire globe before we reach our destination. The long way is looking for God and the Kingdom of Heaven without, somewhere out there. The new and direct way is to go within where God and the Kingdom of Heaven reside. It is our choice which way we decide to go.

His Passion

Christ did not come to suffer and die for our sins. We killed Him because of our sins. We are excellent at justifying our actions instead of taking responsibility for them. While Judas betrayed Christ for 30 pieces of silver, we are betraying Him by refusing to open our eyes fearing that we might see the light. We shut our ears fearing that we might hear the truth. We harden our hearts fearing that we might understand and have compassion.

Why is it that we murder those who come to help us? Why do we persecute our teachers and servants? Not only do we kill our messengers of peace, we eliminate any reminders that they might leave behind. We, not only killed Christ, we burned any writings that tell the truth. We persecuted those who proclaimed a message contrary to what we wanted to hear. When Jesus raised Lazarus from the dead, the priesthood sought not only to kill Jesus, but Lazarus as well. They did not want any witnesses proclaiming the deeds of Christ. No reminders, please.

> *When the large crowd of the Jews learned that Jesus was there, they came, not only on account of him but also to see Lazarus, whom he had raised from the dead. So the chief priests made plans to put Lazarus to death as well, because on account of him many of the Jews were going away and believing in Jesus. John12:9-11*

This is not surprising. Our actions reflect our beliefs and the deities we worship. Not only our gods are in our image, we are in the image of the gods we worship. Just as we killed Christ, the God of the Old Testament sought to kill his own prophet as well —Moses.

> *And it came to pass by the way in the inn, that the LORD met him, and sought to kill him (Moses). Exod 4:24*

Perhaps we kill our prophets so as not to have a reminder of what **we are** compared to what **we can be**.

His Death and Resurrection

Christ did not die on the cross. His physical body did. The physical body is the temple in which the Christ Consciousness resides. This consciousness that is the Christ never dies. Once the spiritual aspect of a person leaves the body, the body dies and disintegrates.

Christ died and was buried as a physical body. He was resurrected purely as a spiritual body. The spiritual body can appear and disappear at will. It can also go through walls.

> *For in the resurrection they neither marry nor are given in marriage, but are like angels in heaven. Matt 22:30*

No angel in heaven has a physical body. Angels are spiritual beings with spiritual bodies only.

Resurrection is the ultimate form of spirituality. It is when one dies physically and is reborn spiritually.

> *Nicodemus said to him, "How can a man be born when he is old? Can he enter a second time into his mother's womb and be born?" Jesus answered, "Truly, truly, I say to you, unless one is born of water and the Spirit, he cannot enter the kingdom of God. That which is born of the flesh is flesh, and that which is born of the Spirit is spirit. Do not marvel that I said to you, 'You must be born again.' The wind blows where it wishes, and you hear its sound, but you do not know where it comes from or where it goes. So it is with everyone who is born of the Spirit." John 3:4-8*

His Ascension

Christ's ascension signifies the completion of His mission. His work was accomplished. Ours is just beginning.

Why the life of Jesus Christ as a Parable?

- Our ultimate evolution is an unfoldment to be Christlike—loving, caring, compassionate and peaceful.
- Unless our eyes open, we cannot see the light.
- Unless our ears are clear, we cannot hear the truth.
- Unless our hearts are compassionate, we cannot feel love.
- Christ showed us how we can have peace on Earth and how we can transform our earth into a heaven of our choosing.
- He wanted to teach us the value of humility by example.

- He wanted us to know what kind of future lies ahead if we only follow His example.
- We are born with talents, skills, and abilities. These are our gifts.
- Suffering is a part of life. It is due to ignorance, ours or someone else's.
- The physical body will die, but we do not have to die if we are reborn spiritually.
- Once we complete our mission, we too will ascend into the higher realms.
- Christ was never a king; not king of the Jews or the king of Israel. His Kingdom was not earthly, but heavenly and spiritual.

Jesus answered, My kingdom is not of this world: if my kingdom were of this world, then would my servants fight, that I should not be delivered to the Jews: but now is my kingdom not from hence. John 18:36

He makes it clear that not only His Kingdom was not of this world, but that He himself did not belong to this material world. His world was spiritual.

He said to them, "You are from below; I am from above. You are of this world; I am not of this world. John 8:23

We, too, are like Christ. Our bodies are of earth, while our Inner Spiritual Self is of heaven.

THE LAST SUPPER AS A PARABLE

Christ knew when His Last Supper was. Unfortunately for us, we have no idea when our last supper will be. It could have been last night. —Shahan Shammas

The Parable

And when the hour came, he reclined at table, and the apostles with him. And he said to them, "I have earnestly desired to eat this Passover with you before I suffer. For I tell you I will not eat it until it is fulfilled in the kingdom of God." And he took a cup, and when he had given thanks he said, "Take this, and divide it among yourselves. For I tell you that from now on I will not drink of the fruit of the vine until the kingdom of God comes." And he took bread, and when he had given thanks, he broke it and gave it to them, saying, "This is my body, which is given for you. Do this in remembrance of me." And likewise the cup after they had eaten, saying, "This cup that is poured out for you is the new covenant in my blood. But behold, the hand of him who betrays me is with me on the table. For the Son of Man goes as it has been determined, but woe to that man by whom he is betrayed!" And they began to question one another, which of them it could be who was going to do this. Luke 22:14-23

Christianity is a beautiful ethical system to live by. It is one of the most noble religions and if its tenants are applied to daily living, our earth will transform into a heaven. There will be peace, brotherhood and sisterhood and there will be an abundance for all.

The last supper holds one of the greatest secrets of Christianity. To unravel it requires a pure heart, childish sincerity, an attentive mind and a compassionate heart. Humanity, at its current stage of unfoldment lacks all of these. We have advanced technology, yet our morals and spirituality are at an infant's level. We have a long way to go. Our nature is still barbaric. We are not yet worthy to claim the deepest secrets of Christianity. First and foremost, we must stop killing other humans as if they do not matter. We must stop abusing our technology at the expense of the weak and defenseless. We must repent from our savage ways, make an about face and adopt the gentle and humane teachings of Christ.

The setting

The Passover with the Disciples

> *Then came the day of Unleavened Bread, on which the Passover lamb had to be sacrificed. So Jesus sent Peter and John, saying, "Go and prepare the Passover for us, that we may eat it." They said to him, "Where will you have us prepare it?" He said to them, "Behold, when you have entered the city, a man carrying a jar of water will meet you. Follow him into the house that he enters and tell the master of the house, 'The Teacher says to you, Where is the guest room, where I may eat the Passover with my disciples?' And he will show you a large upper room furnished; prepare it there." And they went and found it just as he had told them, and they prepared the Passover. Luke 22:7-13*

Reading the three instances of The Last Supper in the gospels, it becomes clear that something very special is afoot. To prepare for it, Jesus asked Peter and John to go into the city and look for a man carrying a jar of water. They are to enter a house and ask the master where the guest room is so they can prepare for the Passover.

Who is this man carrying a jar of water?

How did Jesus know where and when that man will be in the city?

How did Jesus know about the upper, furnished guest room?

Is it possible that both the man carrying the jar of water and the master of the house were secret followers of Christ? Is it possible that Jesus knew of the guest room because He had seen it and in fact had met there before? Is it possible that this house is one of the secret places where Jesus met and taught openly His message of true "salvation?" Obviously, the owner of the house knew who Christ was and was willing to comply. This is a clear indication that he was one His followers.

Preparation

In preparation for the last supper, Christ demonstrated what was expected of us before we can glean the hidden secrets of His teachings.

Jesus Washes the Disciples' Feet

> *Now before the Feast of the Passover, when Jesus knew that his hour had come to depart out of this world to the Father, having loved his own who were in the world, he loved them to the end. During supper, when the devil had already put it into the heart of Judas Iscariot, Simon's son, to betray him, Jesus, knowing that the Father had given*

all things into his hands, and that he had come from God and was going back to God, rose from supper. He laid aside his outer garments, and taking a towel, tied it around his waist. Then he poured water into a basin and began to wash the disciples' feet and to wipe them with the towel that was wrapped around him. He came to Simon Peter, who said to him, "Lord, do you wash my feet?" Jesus answered him, "What I am doing you do not understand now, but afterward you will understand." Peter said to him, "You shall never wash my feet." Jesus answered him, "If I do not wash you, you have no share with me." Simon Peter said to him, "Lord, not my feet only but also my hands and my head!" Jesus said to him, "The one who has bathed does not need to wash, except for his feet, but is completely clean. And you are clean, but not every one of you." For he knew who was to betray him; that was why he said, "Not all of you are clean."

When he had washed their feet and put on his outer garments and resumed his place, he said to them, "Do you understand what I have done to you? You call me Teacher and Lord, and you are right, for so I am. If I then, your Lord and Teacher, have washed your feet, you also ought to wash one another's feet. For I have given you an example, that you also should do just as I have done to you. Truly, truly, I say to you, a servant is not greater than his master, nor is a messenger greater than the one who sent him. If you know these things, blessed are you if you do them. I am not speaking of all of you; I know whom I have chosen. But the Scripture will be fulfilled, 'He who ate my bread has lifted his heel against me.' I am telling you this now, before it takes place, that when it does take place you may believe that I am he. Truly, truly, I say to you, whoever receives the one I send receives me, and whoever receives me receives the one who sent me." John13:1-20

Christ is the master and the lord, yet in preparation He washed the feet of His disciples. He put a towel on His waist (symbol of readiness to serve), got water and a basin and began to wash His disciples' feet. He did this to set an example of how we should treat each other as a way of life, a life of compassionate service.

Imagine what the world would be like if our leaders considered their positions of authority as an opportunity to serve instead of to rule over us. What would happen if our leaders *seriously* considered and adopted the following adage?

> *Whoever humbles himself like this child is the greatest in the kingdom of heaven. Matt 18:4*

Or,

> *The greatest among you shall be your servant. Matt 23:11*

What a world this would be!

Once Christ demonstrated, by example, what He expected from His followers, He was ready to reveal to them His greatest secret —His ultimate message.

The Hidden Meaning of the Last Supper

The bread

The bread has already gone through a transformation. It was flour before it turned into dough through the action of yeast and fermentation. Therefore, bread is a transformed nutrient.

In a sense, Christ is the bread, specifically, His teachings are the bread we need for nourishment.

> *Jesus said to them, "I am the bread of life; whoever comes to me shall not hunger, and whoever believes in me shall never thirst. John 6:35.*

And he who eats this bread, Christ's teachings, will never hunger again.

Bread is the staff of life. It is basic nourishment. This nourishment is not only for the physical body, it must be for the spiritual body as well. That is why Christ, in the Lord's prayer, wants us to ask for our daily bread.

"Give us this day our daily bread," Matt 6:11

This daily bread is not the physical nourishment that we need. Rather, it is the challenges and difficulties we must overcome so we may grow spiritually. These are what nourish the soul.

> But he answered, "It is written, "'Man shall not live by bread alone, but by every word that comes from the mouth of God.'" Matt 4:4

Breaking the bread

Christ broke the bread into small pieces and gave each disciple a piece. This bread is a substitute for the body of Christ. This body is a symbolic representation of His spiritual body—His message and teachings. To believe that Christ was referring to His actual physical body would be absurd. Christ is not trying to sacrifice Himself. There is no longer any need for a blood sacrifice. The sacrifice He is offering is metaphorical. The breaking of the bread into many pieces is symbolic of the "yeast" that ferments the dough and leavens it. Each piece of "bread" entering a disciple's body is the one "mustard seed" that grows into a tree and produces thousands of seeds. It is the net cast into the ocean that attracts thousands of fish. It is the precious pearl and treasure that can transform our lives. It is the few loaves of bread that multiply to feed the five thousand.

The following quote proves that by bread, Christ is referring to teachings:

> When the disciples reached the other side, they had forgotten to bring any bread. Jesus said to them, "Watch and beware of the leaven of the Pharisees and Sadducees." And they began discussing it among themselves, saying, "We brought no bread." But Jesus, aware of this, said, "O you of little faith, why are you discussing among yourselves the fact that you have no bread? Do you not yet perceive? Do you not remember the five loaves for the five thousand, and how many baskets you gathered? Or the seven loaves for the four thousand, and how many baskets you gathered? How is it that you fail to understand that I did not speak about bread? Beware of the leaven of the Pharisees and Sadducees." Then they understood that he did not tell them to beware of the leaven of bread, but of the teaching of the Pharisees and Sadducees. Matt 16:5-12

Secret # 1

We must eat the pure "bread of Christ"— His unadulterated teachings in order to grow spiritually.

Christ makes it clear that we must beware of the kind of "bread" or yeast we take in, for the leavening will take place **regardless of the nature of the yeast**. If we take in the "spiritual body of Christ" as our bread and leaven, we will produce an abundance of good deeds. If, on the other hand, we ingest the teachings of the Old, the Pharisees and the Sadducees, then we will end up with ignorance and misguided beliefs.

The wine

Wine is the symbol for blood and the vital life force. It is essential for life. Just like bread that is transformed flour, wine is transformed grape juice. When Christ indicated that the wine was His blood, it is a figure of speech. It simply means that wine is His essential and most important message and teachings.

Drinking the wine

The same way that Christ divided the bread (multiplied), He divided up the wine by having each disciple drink some of it. Drinking wine is the same as eating the bread. It is ingesting an essential aspect of Christ. Once imbibed, the wine becomes the leaven, the seed, the pearl, the treasure and the net. The human being is transformed into a Holy being, one possessed of the Christ Consciousness.

Secret # 2

The wine is the "blood of Christ"—His most important teachings. This wine is love. We must become love.

If we love at least one individual with our entire being and this love is pure and unselfish, then this love will spiritualize and transform us.

Blessing and giving thanks

The bread that the disciples ate and the wine that they drank were not ordinary. Christ blessed the bread beforehand and He thanked God before offering the wine for drinking. This made the bread and wine consecrated and special.

Secret # 3

We must give thanks and be eternally grateful and appreciative of our blessings.

The disciples were not common, ordinary people. Christ had been teaching them privately for some time. While He taught the general public via parables, He taught His disciples openly and with explanations. Hence, the disciples were already well versed in Christ's teachings and His new message. Each of the disciples, except for Judas, had a well-developed Inner Spiritual Self. This was the disciples' first transformation. This is akin to the grapejuice turning into wine and the flour becoming dough. They were ready for the next stage of transformation.

Through the Last Supper, Christ endeavored to transform His disciples yet again for the second and last time. The first transformation changed their astral bodies into spiritual bodies. By consuming the "bread", the "body" of Christ and by drinking the "wine", the "blood" of Christ, (the most elevated teachings of Christ), the spiritual bodies of the disciples began to slowly transform into the eternal I AM. Progressively, their personal consciousness began to evolve to become the Christ Consciousness. This reached its zenith at Pentecost when the Holy Spirit descended on the disciples. This completed their transformation and the disciples became the masters, Christlike.

Once we are transformed through eating the "body " of Christ and drinking the "blood" of Christ, we, too, will be ready for the Holy Spirit. Once the Holy Spirit descends on us, we become Christlike, functioning as spiritual beings guided by our Inner Spiritual Self. We unite with the I AM and become one with it, and like Christ, we can say:

    I am light!
    I am life!
    I am the way!
    I am the resurrection!
    I and the Father are one. He who has seen me, has seen the Father.

Functioning from the I Am level we are no longer disciples of Christ; we are Christlike.

A New Covenant and a new life in Christ

> *"This cup that is poured out for you is the new covenant in my blood."*

While the first covenant was via circumcision, the new covenant is the symbolic pouring of the blood of Christ as His teachings into cups that only His disciples can drink from. This new covenant is a temple within us that Christ resides in. Christ is not only "the bread" of life, He is also "the true vine." We must remain attached to this true vine at all times.

> *I am the vine; you are the branches. Whoever abides in me and I in him, he it is that bears much fruit, for apart from me you can do nothing. If anyone does not abide in me he is thrown away like a branch and withers; and the branches are gathered, thrown into the fire, and burned. If you abide in me, and my words abide in you, ask whatever you wish, and it will be done for you. John15:5-7*

The temple where Christ resides within us is supported by three pillars.

1. Love

The first pillar is spiritual love. It is an outpouring of genuine care and interest in others. It is forgetting the self and seeing only the other. It is appreciating and celebrating the uniqueness of each individual.

2. Service

The second is to serve genuinely and selflessly without expecting anything in return. It is to feel honored for the opportunity to be of service. It is to enlighten and empower others so that the best of what is buried within them will shine forth.

3. Knowledge

We must live a life of love and service based on knowledge—knowing ourselves, loving ourselves and expressing ourselves. Our light must shine from the mountaintops.

There is no better way to live than to know, to love and to express ourselves through service. These are the most rewarding life experiences we can have.

Personalizing the Parable

Washing the feet

When I was a young boy in Aleppo, Syria, I clearly remember the Syriac Orthodox Church I used to attend and the washing of the feet of anyone who wanted. This was done on a Thursday evening prior to Easter. I had my feet washed by our priest. Back then, I never understood the significance of washing feet. Traditionally, the feet are the dirtiest part of the body because they are used for walking and touching the ground. The washing of the feet is not about removing dirt. It is about the display of utmost humility when done sincerely by a high official. The idea behind Christ washing His disciples' feet is to teach us that, even though He is the master, He is also the servant. He wants to impart the equally important lesson of **humility.**

Service and Humility

I have known a few great people who were the epitome of service and humility. These individuals were humble without pretense. They not only knew who they were, but also who everyone else was. They genuinely felt honored to be in another's presence. Service for them was an opportunity to pour out love and appreciation for others. Humility cannot be feigned. Mock humility is easy to detect. Genuine humility is from the heart and is all encompassing.

Why the Parable?

- To reveal the greatest secret of Christianity.
- To know what the body of Christ is.
- To knowing what the blood of Christ is.
- To express gratitude.
- To reveal that service and humility are the way.
- To emphasize the birth of the *new* covenant founded on Love, Service and Knowledge.

* * * * *

The Last Supper from Other Sources

Gospel of Matthew

Now as they were eating, Jesus took bread, and after blessing it broke it and gave it to the disciples, and said, "Take, eat; this is my body." And he took a cup, and when he had given thanks he gave it to them, saying, "Drink of it, all of you, for this is my blood of the covenant, which is poured out for many for the forgiveness of sins. I tell you I will not drink again of this fruit of the vine until that day when I drink it new with you in my Father's kingdom." Matt 26:26-29

Gospel of Mark

And as they were eating, he took bread, and after blessing it broke it and gave it to them, and said, "Take; this is my body." And he took a cup, and when he had given thanks he gave it to them, and they all drank of it. And he said to them, "This is my blood of the covenant, which is poured out for many. Truly, I say to you, I will not drink again of the fruit of the vine until that day when I drink it new in the kingdom of God." Mark 14:22-25

The Last Supper according to 1 Cor.

For I received from the Lord what I also delivered to you, that the Lord Jesus on the night when he was betrayed took bread, and when he had given thanks, he broke it, and said, "This is my body which is for you. Do this in remembrance of me." In the same way also he took the cup, after supper, saying, "This cup is the new covenant in my blood. Do this, as often as you drink it, in remembrance of me." For as often as you eat this bread and drink the cup, you proclaim the Lord's death until he comes. 1Cor 11:23-26

The Passover with the Disciples *(Matthew)*

Now on the first day of Unleavened Bread the disciples came to Jesus, saying, "Where will you have us prepare for you to eat the Passover?" He said, "Go into the city to a certain man and say to him, 'The Teacher says, My time is at hand. I will keep the Passover at your house with my disciples.'" And the disciples did as Jesus had directed them, and they prepared the Passover. Matt 26: 17-19

The Passover with the Disciples *(Mark)*

And on the first day of Unleavened Bread, when they sacrificed the Passover lamb, his disciples said to him, "Where will you have us go and prepare for you to eat the Passover?" And he sent two of his disciples and said to them, "Go into the city, and a man carrying a jar of water will meet you. Follow him, and wherever he enters, say to the master of the house, 'The Teacher says, Where is my guest room, where I may eat the Passover with my disciples?' And he will show you a large upper room furnished and ready; there prepare for us." And the disciples set out and went to the city and found it just as he had told them, and they prepared the Passover. Mark 14:12-16

SUMMARY

We know why Christ had to use parables. But why would He use these specific parables? What was His intention? What was He trying to convey through these parables? What is important about these specific parables?

There are at least five main themes that traverse throughout these parables:

1. We are loved.
2. We are in a vineyard.
3. The Kingdom of God is within.
4. We are done with the Old.
5. We are invited to a wedding feast.

1. We are loved

The three parables of **The Prodigal Son**, **The Lost Sheep** and **The Lost Coin** make it amply clear that we are loved beyond measure. What does this mean?

For one thing, this love is unconditional. We are loved regardless of what we have done or did not do. We are loved just for who we are—children of the Father. Because we are loved dearly, we are expected to give something in return to demonstrate our appreciation. We cannot disappoint those who love us. We must reciprocate somehow. We do this by being proactive and serious about growing, improving and progressively using more of our gifts (talents, skills and abilities) to do the work of our Father which is to grow spiritually.

Being loved for who we are negates the belief that we are sinful and have been born with an original sin. Being loved unconditionally also implies that there is no need for anyone to sacrifice their life for us. Hence, Christ did not die for our sins. He died, or rather we killed Him, because of our sins. Our sins are ignorance, blindness, resistance to change, deafness and the hardening of our hearts.

2. We are in a vineyard

We are laborers in the vineyard of life. We are given tools (gifts) to work with. These are our talents, skills and abilities. We have two options: we could ignore our gifts (bury them for no return), or we could invest them for a multi-fold return. The more industrious we are, the more we will end up with. Using mental and spiritual tools will enhance our returns. Being lazy (idle) is not an option. Cooperating with others speeds up our progress.

3. The Kingdom of God is within

The Kingdom of God is within us as a seed that must be nurtured and allowed to grow and blossom. This Kingdom is a particular form of knowledge. With the proper knowledge, we can make the right decisions that place us on the accelerated path to know who we are, and to love and express ourselves.

4. We are done with the Old

Christ makes it clear that the Old ended with John the Baptist and the New began with Him. We are to leave the Old behind and embrace the New. The New is all that we need for an abundant life. No more Old Testament for the followers of Christ.

5. We are invited to a wedding feast

The invitations to a wedding feast are out. Most will make excuses and refuse to attend. Few will accept the invitation and come. Christ wants us to look at our lives as a wedding celebration. We have been gifted an enormous amount. We must open our eyes and count our blessings. The more appreciative we are of our free gifts, the more will come our way. What we dwell on we empower.

Many who attend weddings are interested in eating, drinking and socializing. This is fine. However, as Christ demonstrated, there is another reason for attending the wedding feast. We must dress appropriately. In other words, we must have the right attitude. Additionally, there is a shortage of wine at this wedding. This is a perceived crisis. It is our responsibility, if we choose to assume it, to provide the needed wine by transmuting water into wine. In other words, finding a creative solution to the crisis via transformation. By converting our challenges into opportunities, we defuse the crisis and we gain mastery.

* * * * *

To glean the hidden reason why Christ used these particular parables, we will look at each parable individually. We will unravel the underlying reason for its inclusion in the Gospels. We will focus only on the main points.

Parable of The Lamp

We should never forget that we are the light of the world. An unlit lamp is useless as a source of light. We must be like a lighthouse constantly shining our light. Our light makes a difference. It dispels darkness.

Parable of The Speck and Log

Everyone has something in their eyes. No one is perfect. We

cannot see what is in another's eye, unless we first clear what is in ours. The speck in someone else's eye is perhaps more of an irritant to us than to them. We should ignore it. Many of our leaders have logs in their eyes. They are blind. We need not follow them. Instead, we should focus on what we need to do to remove our blinders and see clearly.

Parable of The New Cloth on an Old Garment

We need to put the Old behind us. Christ is the New wine. Imbibing His teachings will nourish us spiritually. We must keep these teachings pure and pristine without contaminating them with the Old.

Parable of The Divided Kingdom

Good and evil are forces residing in our hearts and minds. Good and evil acts require intent which only humans exhibit. We must stop blaming Satan for our evil deeds. We are responsible for all that we do. We can exercise our freedom of choice and choose wisely.

Parable of The Sower

We are bombarded by external seeds (ideas, advertisements, etc.). It is best to evaluate each one. We should practice being our own Sower of seeds. We should select our seeds carefully, plant them in our hearts and minds and act with our eyes wide open.

Parable of The Weeds Among the Wheat

The worst weeds are those growing in our hearts and minds. By dwelling on the "the good seeds" in our lives, we empower them and, at the same time, we starve the weeds.

Parable of The Kingdom of Heaven

The Kingdom of Heaven within us is a specific knowledge. Knowing that we have a choice is of the utmost importance.

Making the correct choices sets us on the right path. By choosing, we decide our present and determine our future.

Parable of The Heart of Man

The heart and the mind are powerful breeding grounds. They can breed good or evil. Only what comes out of the heart can defile us.

Parable of The Lost Sheep

We are valued beyond measure. Most of us are like lost sheep floundering through life. We must wake up the shepherd within and listen to its promptings.

Parable of The Unforgiving Servant

We must forgive before we are forgiven. Forgiveness must be from the heart. It helps us as much as those we forgive.

Parable of The Laborers in the Vineyard

We are the laborers in the vineyard of life. It does not matter when we begin laboring, as long as we begin in earnest and give it our best.

Parable of The Prodigal Son

We are the Prodigal Son. We need to find our way back home. A celebration is waiting for us once we are home.

Parable of The Tenant Farmers

Christ is **the Stone** and His teachings are the foundation on which we should base our lives. The only way we can inherit the Father's abundance is to become a Child of God ourselves.

Parable of The Wedding Feast

We are invited to a wedding where a feast is prepared for us. We must stop making excuses and accept the invitation. To be a worthy guest, we must dress accordingly. Our eyes must be open. Our ears must be clear. Our hearts must be sensitive and compassionate.

Parable of The Barren Fig Tree

We are expected to be productive. Idleness is not tolerated.

Parable of The Wicked Servant

Life is an opportunity to prove ourselves. We can choose to be wicked or good servants. Our actions have consequences.

Parable of The Ten Virgins

We must stay awake. Opportunity might knock at any moment and we must be ready to take advantage of it. We must prepare for any eventuality.

Parable of The Talents

Everyone without exception is gifted with some talents. We are expected to employ these talents for a good return. If we are diligent, we can at least double our investments by the end of our lives. Becoming skilled mentally and spiritually ensures that we will increase our rate of return.

Parable of The Good Samaritan

To be able to help another should be viewed as a privilege. We have ups and downs. It is wonderful to have someone give us a hand when we are down and for us to aid another when they are down. Our neighbor is anyone who crosses our path and needs a helping hand regardless of race or ethnicity.

Parable of The Friend at Midnight

Life is full of surprises and midnight is when the unexpected happens. We must face our challenges with boldness, courage and creativity. The gift of the Holy Spirit is the best gift we can ever have.

Parable of The Rich Fool

We could die at any moment, so greed does not pay. It is best to accumulate treasures that do not spoil such as knowledge and enduring relationships.

Parable of The Invited Guests

Christ is admonishing us to live as if we are invited guests to a wedding. We should appreciate our opportunity to be alive and celebrate. We should not seek honor. Rather, if we deserve it, allow others to honor us.

Parable of The Lost Coin

With this parable Christ is imprinting on us that we are the lost silver coin. To find our way, we must light our inner lamp, clean our house and seek diligently.

Parable of The Rich Man and Lazarus

Life on Earth is temporary. Soon we will die and have a chance to evaluate our actions and their consequences. We will feel anguish and regret over our "bad" actions and we will feel gratified and satisfied over our "good" actions. We are expected to share the excess from our wealth with those less fortunate.

Parable of The Persistent Widow

At times, persistence, tenacity and determination are a must. We should never give up or lose heart. We can move mountains through faith and knowledge.

Parable of The Pharisee and the Tax Collector

We need to be sincere and humble. What matters is purity of heart, not social stranding or appearance. If we exalt ourselves, there is nowhere to go but down. If we humble ourselves, there is nowhere to go but up.

The Life of Jesus Christ as a Parable

Our ultimate evolution is an unfoldment to be Christlike—loving, caring, compassionate and peaceful. Unless our eyes are open, we cannot see the light. Unless our ears are clear, we cannot hear the truth. Unless our hearts are compassionate, we cannot feel love.

Christ showed us how we can have peace on Earth and how we can transform our earth into a heaven of our choosing. He wanted to teach us the value of humility by example. He wanted to show us what kind of future lies ahead if only we follow His example.

We are born with talents, skills and abilities. These gifts are free. Suffering is a part of life. It is due mostly to ignorance. The physical body will die, but we do not have to die if we are reborn spiritually. Once we complete our mission, we too will ascend into the higher realms.

Parable of The Last Supper

The Last Supper reveals some of the greatest secrets of Christianity. We discover what the body of Christ is. We learn what the blood of Christ is. We realize the value of being thankful.

Christ, by washing the feet of His disciples, revealed the virtues of service and humility. It is best to be humble rather than seek lofty positions from where we can fall.

The Last Supper emphasizes the birth of the *new* covenant founded on the three pillars of Love, Service and Knowledge.

Christ was never an earthly king—not king of the Jews or the king of Israel. His Kingdom was not earthly. It was heavenly and spiritual.

CONCLUSION

Now that the secret (private) teachings of Christ have been revealed, what are we going to do with them? We can ignore them, but then the life, passion and death of Christ would have been for naught. The other choice is to adopt them, incorporate them into our being and express them in our daily living.

The Christ Consciousness is the Light of the World. It can dispel all forms of darkness, from our hearts and from the world. Christ came to usher in a New Age—the Age of Enlightenment. This can only happen if we adopt spirituality as a way of life.

To usher in the New we must let go of the Old. Here is what is **In** and what's **Out:**

OUT	IN
We are not born in sin. We can live in sin if we ignore the dictates of our conscience.	We can choose to live in grace where sin has no power over us. *For sin will have no dominion over you, since you are not under law but under grace.* Rom 6:14
Hundreds of	We live our life guided by love

commandments regulating every aspect of our lives.	and our conscience.
The concept that some are chosen while the rest are less important.	We are equally loved and valued by Our Father who would welcome us, His Prodigal Children, with open arms once we decide to head back home.
Wanton killings, murders, aggression and genocide of the weak and powerless.	Appreciation of differences, respect for diversity and compassion toward those less fortunate than us.
Revenge. An eye for an eye mentality.	Tolerance and forgiveness. Finding solutions that work for the benefit of all concerned.
Wars and barbaric behavior. Raw, aggressive competition.	Peace and enlightened behavior. Cooperation, friendly competition and joint ventures.
The physical and the material as our main focus.	Seeking the spiritual first, then the material will follow automatically.
Accumulating and storing treasures on Earth.	Accumulating spiritual treasures—wisdom, knowledge and understanding.

The vices.	The virtues.
Fear of The Lord as the beginning of wisdom.	Love of God as wisdom.
Eyes that do not see. Ears that do not hear. Hearts that do not feel.	Eyes wide open. Ears clear and attentive. Hearts full of love and compassion.
Privilege.	Earned respect.
Baptism by water.	Baptism by the fire of daily living through hardships, difficulties and challenges.
Protecting the life of the unborn while ignoring the death of young adults wasted in wars.	All life is valuable regardless of age.
Taking our everyday gifts for granted.	Appreciation of all that we have.
Pride.	Humility.

APPENDIX A

The Messiah Prophecies

The Gospel writers tried desperately to show that Christ was the expected Messiah. They searched the Old Testament for prophecies regarding the Messiah and they not only inserted those passages into the Gospels, but they also made sure that Jesus performed the expected acts so that He would be thought of as the expected Messiah.

The meaning of passages taken out of context can easily be manipulated. We can easily be fooled as to what they mean unless we read a chapter or two before and after those passages. This is what happened to the Gospels. We are led to believe that those inserted prophecies are about Jesus. As you will see, none of them are. They are about the people of old and their immediate circumstances.

Jesus was not the Messiah. There are no prophecies in the Old Testament about Jesus. The insertions in the New Testament are forgeries.

Was Jesus a descendant of David?

To prove that Jesus is the expected Messiah, the Gospels attempt to demonstrate that Jesus was a descendant of King David. This expectation comes from Jeremiah. Here is the original quote:

> "Behold, the days are coming, declares the LORD, when I will raise up for David a righteous Branch, and he shall reign as king and deal wisely, and shall execute justice and righteousness in the land. In his days Judah will be saved,

> and Israel will dwell securely. And this is the name by which he will be called: 'The LORD is our righteousness.' Jeremiah 23:5-6

It is obvious that this prophecy cannot apply to Jesus.

Jesus was born of the Holy Spirit through Mary. Additionally, it was Joseph who was from the house of David. Joseph had no part in Jesus' birth.

Matthew traces the lineage of **Joseph** to King David, but Joseph was not the biological father of Jesus.

> *The book of the genealogy of Jesus Christ, the son of David, the son of Abraham. Matt 1:1*
>
> *and Jacob the father of Joseph the husband of Mary, of whom Jesus was born, who is called Christ. Matt 1:16*
>
> *But as he considered these things, behold, an angel of the Lord appeared to him in a dream, saying, "Joseph, son of David, do not fear to take Mary as your wife, for that which is conceived in her is from the Holy Spirit. Matt 1:20*

So does Luke.

> *In the sixth month the angel Gabriel was sent from God to a city of Galilee named Nazareth, to a virgin betrothed to a man whose name was Joseph, of the house of David. And the virgin's name was Mary. Luke 1:26-27*
>
> *He will be great and will be called the Son of the Most High. And the Lord God will give to him the throne of his father David, and he will reign over the house of Jacob forever, and of his kingdom there will be no end." Luke 1:32-33*

Christ never reigned as king over the Jews, Israel or anybody else.

Did Herod kill the children?

> *Then Herod, when he saw that he was mocked of the wise men, was exceeding wroth, and sent forth, and slew all the children that were in Bethlehem, and in all the coasts thereof, from two years old and under, according to the time which he had diligently enquired of the wise men. Then was fulfilled that which was spoken by Jeremy the prophet, saying, In Rama was there a voice heard, lamentation, and weeping, and great mourning, Rachel weeping for her children, and would not be comforted, because they are not. Matt 2:16-18*

Here is the original quote from Jeremiah:

> *Thus says the LORD: "A voice is heard in Ramah, lamentation and bitter weeping. Rachel is weeping for her children; she refuses to be comforted for her children, because they are no more." Jer 31:15*

This quote is regarding lamentations in **Ramah** during ancient times, not around Bethlehem where Jesus was born.

> *Ramah (from Hebrew: "height" was, according to the Hebrew Bible, a city in ancient Israel in the land allocated to the tribe of Benjamin. It was located near Gibeon and Mizpah to the West, Gibeah to the South, and Geba to the East.*
>
> *Ramah has been commonly identified with modern al-Ram, about 8 kilometers (5.0 mi) north of Jerusalem. Na'aman preferred to identify Ramah with the nearby site of Nabi Samwil. Wikipedia*

The idea that anyone could kill innocent children is beyond barbaric and is abhorrent. But there is precedent to this in the Old Testament when Yahweh ordered the massacre of the first born of the Egyptians.

> *At midnight the LORD struck down all the firstborn in the land of Egypt, from the firstborn of Pharaoh who sat*

> on his throne to the firstborn of the captive who was in the dungeon, and all the firstborn of the livestock. And Pharaoh rose up in the night, he and all his servants and all the Egyptians. And there was a great cry in Egypt, for there was not a house where someone was not dead. Exodus 12:29-30

Was Jesus from Nazareth?

> And he came and dwelt in a city called Nazareth: that it might be fulfilled which was spoken by the prophets, He shall be called a Nazarene. Matt 2:23

There are no references in the Old Testament that Jesus was expected to come from Nazareth. We have no idea what Matthew is referring to.

What does this refer to?

> Now when Jesus had heard that John was cast into prison, he departed into Galilee; And leaving Nazareth, he came and dwelt in Capernaum, which is upon the sea coast, in the borders of Zabulon and Nephthalim: That it might be fulfilled which was spoken by Esaias the prophet, saying, The land of Zabulon, and the land of Nephthalim, by the way of the sea, beyond Jordan, Galilee of the Gentiles; The people which sat in darkness saw great light; and to them which sat in the region and shadow of death light is sprung up. Matt 4:12-16

I have no idea how this is a prophecy or how it relates to Christ. Seeing a great light or light springing up has no relation to Christ.

Did Christ take over our infirmities and bear our sickness?

> That evening they brought to him many who were oppressed by demons, and he cast out the spirits with a

> word and healed all who were sick. This was to fulfill what was spoken by the prophet Isaiah: "He took our illnesses and bore our diseases." Matt 8:16-17

Did Christ take over our illnesses and bear our diseases?

Here is the reference in Isaiah.

> *Surely he has borne our griefs and carried our sorrows; yet we esteemed him stricken, smitten by God, and afflicted. But he was pierced for our transgressions; he was crushed for our iniquities; upon him was the chastisement that brought us peace, and with his wounds we are healed.*
> *All we like sheep have gone astray; we have turned—every one—to his own way; and the LORD has laid on him the iniquity of us all. Isa 53:4-6*

The passage above is in regards to a suffering servant. According to the Internet: "Christians generally identifying the servant as Jesus Christ, while Jews see it as referring to the nation of Israel or a righteous remnant."

Was Jesus the beloved servant?

> *But the Pharisees went out and conspired against him, how to destroy him. Jesus, aware of this, withdrew from there. And many followed him, and he healed them all and ordered them not to make him known. This was to fulfill what was spoken by the prophet Isaiah:*
>
> *"Behold, my servant whom I have chosen, my beloved with whom my soul is well pleased. I will put my Spirit upon him, and he will proclaim justice to the Gentiles. He will not quarrel or cry aloud, nor will anyone hear his voice in the streets; a bruised reed he will not break, and a smoldering wick he will not quench, until he brings justice to victory; and in his name the Gentiles will hope." Matt 12:14-21*

Here is the original quote:

> *Behold my servant, whom I uphold, my chosen, in whom my soul delights; I have put my Spirit upon him; he will bring forth justice to the nations.*
> *He will not cry aloud or lift up his voice, or make it heard in the street;*
> *a bruised reed he will not break, and a faintly burning wick he will not quench; he will faithfully bring forth justice. He will not grow faint or be discouraged (or bruised) till he has established justice in the earth; and the coastlands wait for his law. Isaiah 42:1-4*

In the previous chapter, chapter 41, it is clear who this servant of the Lord is. It is not the Messiah. It is Israel:

> *But you, Israel, my servant, Jacob, whom I have chosen, the offspring of Abraham, my friend; you whom I took from the ends of the earth, and called from its farthest corners, saying to you, "You are my servant, I have chosen you and not cast you off"; Isa 41:8-9*

Is this prophecy about Jesus?

> *Therefore speak I to them in parables: because they seeing see not; and hearing they hear not, neither do they understand. And in them is fulfilled the prophecy of Esaias, which saith,* **By hearing ye shall hear, and shall not understand; and seeing ye shall see, and shall not perceive: For this people's heart is waxed gross, and their ears are dull of hearing, and their eyes they have closed; lest at any time they should see with their eyes, and hear with their ears, and should understand with their heart, and should be converted, and I should heal them. Matt 13:13-15**

Here is the original quote:

> *And he said, "Go, and say to this people: "'Keep on hearing, but do not understand; keep on seeing, but do*

> not perceive.' Make the heart of this people dull, and their ears heavy, and blind their eyes; lest they see with their eyes, and hear with their ears, and understand with their hearts, and turn and be healed." Then I said, "How long, O Lord?" And he said:

> "Until cities lie waste without inhabitant, and houses without people, and the land is a desolate waste, and the LORD removes people far away, and the forsaken places are many in the midst of the land. And though a tenth remain in it, it will be burned again, like a terebinth or an oak, whose stump remains when it is felled." Isa 6:9-13

Obviously, this is about the time prior to the Babylonian captivity.

Was Jesus a king?

> This took place to fulfill what was spoken by the prophet, saying, "Say to the daughter of Zion, 'Behold, your king is coming to you, humble, and mounted on a donkey, on a colt, the foal of a beast of burden.'" Matt 21:4-5

Here is the original quote:

> Rejoice greatly, O daughter of Zion! Shout aloud, O daughter of Jerusalem! Behold, your king is coming to you; righteous and having salvation is he, humble and mounted on a donkey, on a colt, the foal of a donkey.
> I will cut off the chariot from Ephraim and the war horse from Jerusalem; and the battle bow shall be cut off, and he shall speak peace to the nations; his rule shall be from sea to sea, and from the River to the ends of the earth. Zechariah 9:9-10

Jesus was never a king. His rule never extended from sea to sea. Looking at the quotation in its entirety, it is clear that this prophecy is not about Jesus.

> Now it was the day of Preparation of the Passover. It was about the sixth hour. He said to the Jews, "Behold your

> King!" They cried out, "Away with him, away with him, crucify him!" Pilate said to them, "Shall I crucify your King?" The chief priests answered, "We have no king but Caesar." John 19:14-15

Is this prophecy about Judas?

> Then was fulfilled that which was spoken by Jeremy the prophet, saying, And they took the thirty pieces of silver, the price of him that was valued, whom they of the children of Israel did value; And gave them for the potter's field, as the Lord appointed me. Matt 27:9-10

There is no such quote in Jeremiah. The closest we can find to this quote is in Zechariah. Here is the quote:

> So it was annulled on that day, and the sheep traders, who were watching me, knew that it was the word of the LORD. Then I said to them, "If it seems good to you, give me my wages; but if not, keep them." And they weighed out as my wages thirty pieces of silver. Then the LORD said to me, "Throw it to the potter"— the lordly price at which I was priced by them. So I took the thirty pieces of silver and threw them into the house of the LORD, to the potter. Zechariah 11:1213

This quote has nothing to do with Judas.

How about this prophecy?

> And they crucified him, and parted his garments, casting lots: that it might be fulfilled which was spoken by the prophet, **They parted my garments among them, and upon my vesture did they cast lots.** And sitting down they watched him there; And set up over his head his accusation written, THIS IS JESUS THE KING OF THE JEWS. Matt 27:35-37

This quote is from Psalm 22 and it is about king David, not Jesus.

> they divide my garments among them, and for my clothing they cast lots. Ps 22:18

Were two thieves crucified with Jesus?

> And with him they crucify two thieves; the one on his right hand, and the other on his left. And the scripture was fulfilled, which saith, And he was numbered with the transgressors. Mark 15:27-28

This quote is from Isaiah 53 and it is about the suffering Servant of the Lord, not the Messiah.

> Therefore I will divide him a portion with the many, and he shall divide the spoil with the strong, because he poured out his soul to death and was numbered with the transgressors; yet he bore the sin of many, and makes intercession for the transgressors. Isa 53:12

Both Matthew and Mark mention the two thieves. John mentions "two others":

> Then two robbers were crucified with him, one on the right and one on the left. Matt 27:38

> And with him they crucified two robbers, one on his right and one on his left. Mark 15:27

> There they crucified him, and with him two others, one on either side, and Jesus between them. John 19:18

Luke distinguishes between the two thieves as one ending up going to heaven while the other does not.

> One of the criminals who were hanged railed at him, saying, "Are you not the Christ? Save yourself and us!" But the other rebuked him, saying, "Do you not fear God, since you are under the same sentence of condemnation? And we indeed justly, for we are receiving the due reward of our deeds; but this man has done nothing wrong." And he said,

> "Jesus, remember me when you come into your kingdom." And he said to him, "Truly, I say to you, today you will be with me in Paradise." Luke 23:39-43

Did Christ carry His own Cross?

> As they went out, they found a man of Cyrene, Simon by name. They compelled this man to carry his cross. Matt 27:32

> And they compelled a passerby, Simon of Cyrene, who was coming in from the country, the father of Alexander and Rufus, to carry his cross. Mark 15:21

> And as they led him away, they seized one Simon of Cyrene, who was coming in from the country, and laid on him the cross, to carry it behind Jesus. Luke 23:26

While Matthew, Mark and Luke state that Simon of Cyrene carried the cross of Jesus, John states that Jesus carried His own cross:

> So he delivered him over to them to be crucified. So they took Jesus, and he went out, bearing his own cross, to the place called The Place of a Skull, which in Aramaic is called Golgotha. There they crucified him, and with him two others, one on either side, and Jesus between them. John 19:16-18

Does this prophecy apply to Jesus?

> Though he had done so many signs before them, they still did not believe in him, so that the word spoken by the prophet Isaiah might be fulfilled:

> "Lord, who has believed what he heard from us, and to whom has the arm of the Lord been revealed?" Therefore they could not believe. For again Isaiah said, "He has blinded their eyes and hardened their heart, lest they see with their eyes, and understand with their heart, and

turn, and I would heal them." Isaiah said these things because he saw his glory and spoke of him. *John 12:37-41*

Here are the original quotes:

Who has believed what he has heard from us? And to whom has the arm of the LORD been revealed? Isa 53:1

They know not, nor do they discern, for he has shut their eyes, so that they cannot see, and their hearts, so that they cannot understand. No one considers, nor is there knowledge or discernment to say, "Half of it I burned in the fire; I also baked bread on its coals; I roasted meat and have eaten. And shall I make the rest of it an abomination? Shall I fall down before a block of wood?" Isa 44:18-19

The above quotes are about the 'folly of' Idolatry and have nothing to do with the Messiah.

Is this prophecy about Jesus?

Whoever hates me hates my Father also. If I had not done among them the works that no one else did, they would not be guilty of sin, but now they have seen and hated both me and my Father. But the word that is written in their Law must be fulfilled: 'They hated me without a cause.' John 15:23-25

The above reference is in Psalm 69:4. It is about King David and not the Messiah.

More in number than the hairs of my head are those who hate me without cause; mighty are those who would destroy me, those who attack me with lies. What I did not steal must I now restore? Ps 69:4

How about this prophecy?

For these things took place that the Scripture might be fulfilled: "Not one of his bones will be broken." And again another Scripture says, "They will look on him whom they

> have pierced." John 19:36-37

The first is from Psalm 34:20. Once again, it is in reference to King David and not the Messiah.

> He keeps all his bones; not one of them is broken. Ps 34:20

The second is from Zechariah 12:10. This quote is about the old days and has nothing to do with the Messiah.

> "And I will pour out on the house of David and the inhabitants of Jerusalem a spirit of grace and pleas for mercy, so that, when they look on me, on him whom they have pierced, they shall mourn for him, as one mourns for an only child, and weep bitterly over him, as one weeps over a firstborn. On that day the mourning in Jerusalem will be as great as the mourning for Hadad-rimmon in the plain of Megiddo. Zechariah 12:10-11

This prophecy is about the house of David who would pierce the LORD. It has nothing to do with a Messiah.

Was Jesus calling Elijah?

> And about the ninth hour Jesus cried out with a loud voice, saying, "Eli, Eli, lema sabachthani?" that is, "My God, my God, why have you forsaken me?" Matt 27:46

The above verse is from Psalms 22:1

> My God, my God, why have you forsaken me? Why are you so far from saving me, from the words of my groaning? O my God, I cry by day, but you do not answer, and by night, but I find no rest. Ps 22:1

These are King David's words.

* * * * *

Why did the Old Testament Become Part of the Christian Bible?

According to professor Bart Ehrman, PhD: (**The Greatest Controversies of Early Chrisitan History**).

One reason is that the early Christians were Jews.

"Another reason that orthodox Christians decided to retain the Old Testament is that it alone provided antiquity for the Christian religion. Unlike the modern world, the world of antiquity valued the ancient over the novel. For a philosophy to be right, it had to be ancient."

* * * * *

Christ, in several parables, made it clear that we cannot mix the Old and the New. We must keep the New pristine. It is time to let go of the Old. The teachings of Christ suffice for a life of peace, joy and abundance. When we have all we need, anything extra is unnecessary baggage. It is best to travel light and unencumbered.

APPENDIX B

The Esoteric Significance of Numbers

Christ referenced several numbers in His parables. These numbers were not haphazard. They were used with intention because they had spiritual meaning and significance.

Numbers 1,2,5 and 10 are used in the parables.

Christ had 12 disciples and at the age of 12, He appeared in the temple and astonished the priesthood.

At the age of 30, Christ was baptized and began His mission.

At the age of 33, Christ was crucified and His earthly mission ended.

His mission lasted 3 years.

Christ was in the tomb for 3 days.

Christ was in the wilderness for 40 days and 40 nights.

Since these numbers are not random, it helps to take a closer look at their hidden significance. I have consulted the book of: ***An Illustrated Encyclopedia of Traditional Symbols*** by J.C. Cooper with some of these meanings.

* * * * *

Zero

Absolute potential. Hidden. Unmanifest. Unlimited. Eternal. The absence of all quality or quantity. The void.

One

Source, unity in multiplicity, oneness. Beginning.

Examples: One God containing a multiplicity of beings. One body containing a multiplicity of cells, tissues, organs and systems

Two

The nature of life, duality representing the opposite ends of the spectrum. Conflict.

Examples: positive and negative, male and female, day and night.

Three

Creativity, the interaction of the positive and the negative giving rise to an offspring containing features from both. $3 = 1 + 2$. Beginning of multiplicity. Imbalance. Trinity. Body, mind and soul. Resolution of conflict.

Examples: On the third day. The three temptations of Christ. The three denials of Peter. The three days of death and resurrection.

Four

Stability. square. Earth. matter. The created world. Solidity. Balance.

Examples: 4 evangelists. 4 rivers of Eden. 4 elements (earth, water, air, fire).

4 seasons.

Five

The human being, microcosm. The pentagon.

Examples: The human body with 2 arms, 2 legs and a head. 5 senses

Six

As above, so below. Completion. Harmony. The number of

stages it takes to complete a function. The road to completion. Fulfillment.

Since many beasts have tails, the number 6 can also mean "beast" as well. Many beasts have 4 legs, a head and a tail.

Example: 6 days of creation.

Seven

Completion of a cycle. Symbol of cosmic and spiritual order and harmony. The macrocosm.

3 + 4 See-Saw between balance and imbalance.

Examples: The 7 vices (anger, avarice, envy, gluttony, pride and sloth), the 7 virtues (faith, hope, love, justice, prudence, temperance, and fortitude), the 7 stages of human development, the 7 tones of music, the 7 days of the week.

Eight

Rebirth, resurrection. The spiritual goal achieved. A new beginning.

Example: the 8 beatitudes

Nine

Completion of three levels: physical, mental and spiritual attainment.

Example: 9 months of gestation for humans

Ten

The perfect number containing all other numbers. Unlimited potential. Divinity.

Example: The 10 virgins

Eleven

Sin, transgression and peril.

Twelve

Completion of a cycle. The spiritualization of the material. The esoteric and exoteric combined. Cosmic order.

Examples: 12 disciples. 12 months of the year. 12 signs of the zodiac.

Thirteen

The number used in divination. It is the number of a witch's coven. It is considered an unlucky number.

Twenty

The symbol of the whole person. It is the total of all fingers and toes.

Forty

Period of trial, tribulation, challenge and difficulty. Initiation. Death and rebirth.

Examples: 40 days in the wilderness. 40 days of flooding.

Fifty

The Great Year. A return to the beginning. A fresh start.

Sixty

Longevity.

Seventy

The allotted span of a human life.

Seventy-Seven

Whatever it takes to fulfill and utterly complete. To do until one is done with. Complete satisfaction.

666

The number (mark) of the Beast. The anti-Christ. Since 6 is the number for beast; 666 stands for triple beast, the ultimate and meanest of them all.

The ancients did not have numbers like we do. They used the

letters of the alphabet to designate numerical values. The first letter, for example will have the value of 1 and so on. According to Professor Bart Ehrman, using gematria, the ancients came up with numerical values for people using their names. The number 666 is the number for Caesar Nero who persecuted early Christians. Spelled differently, the value for Caesar Nero becomes 616.

888

The sacred number of Jesus the Christ.

APPENDIX C

How one book altered the course of my life

Books don't change the world, people change the world, books only change people. — Mario Quintana

Soon after I was stationed at Ft. Meade, Md, I befriended a man from Chicago, IL. His name was J. T. One day, out of the blue, J. T offered me a book as a gift. This book was **<u>The Greatest Salesman in the World</u>** by Og Mandino. I, not only read the book, but I applied the principles stated in the book to my life. In the ensuing months, I purchased and gave away multiple copies of this same book to various people. Since this one book altered the course of my life for the better, I wanted to do the same for as many people as I could. I would like to acquaint you with seven books, any of which can do the same for you and anyone else you care about.

I have labored long and hard to find answers to the perplexing questions of life. My persistence to know inspired me to find answers that satisfy. I made many discoveries, and in the process, seven life altering books were born.

Our lives are short. Our time is valuable. We are gifted with free will. We can choose what we do with our time and our lives. It behooves us to use some of it to cultivate our minds and nurture our souls. These are the treasures that do not spoil.

The greatest gifts we have been given are talents, skills and abilities. These are obvious. What is less obvious are the gifts of time and free will. Unless we make the right choices in life, we do not advance. How or if we use our talents, skills and abilities is a choice; so is developing additional talents, skills and abilities. The quality of our life rests in our hands based on the choices we make and the actions we take.

The easiest way to advance our station in life is to increase our knowledge, but knowledge is not information. The most valuable knowledge is that which stems from experience, ours or someone else's. All of my books are based on experiential knowledge and inspiration. A little investment on your part using what I learned will yield a large return. What do I gain from making this offer?

I live to make a difference in our world. I love our incredibly beautiful planet. I want to see peace, prosperity and joint ventures the world over. My mission is to be a light that dispels darkness in all of its forms: ignorance, rigidity of heart and mind, and intolerance. I want us to have eyes that see, ears that hear and hearts that feel. By writing, teaching and by making these books available to you, I achieve my purpose.

We deserve better and it is up to us. Together, you and I can make a difference. We are all children of a loving God and we are here to do our part. We have a job ahead of us. We must accept our role and do our part.

If I, born in Syria to almost illiterate parents, in a repressive environment whose language isn't even English, am willing to do my part, so can you. We are not powerless. The more we use what we already have, the more will come our way. That is what I discovered, learned and applied in my life. If we wisely do what we now can do, more doors will open up for us. That is a promise and it is a spiritual law.

Learn, teach, serve and be an example. Let your light shine. Do not allow others to dim your light by covering it up through disempowering beliefs, fears or threats of eternal punishment. A loving God never, ever punishes His children. God only loves.

I urge you to invest in yourself. You are valuable and your contribution is needed. It is essential that we each do our part. Consider acquiring these seven books. They will not only enrich your life, but also the lives of anyone else who might happen to read them because of you.

* * * * *

Seven Books to Set a New Course in Life

By Shahan Shammas. Available at Amazon.com

1. A Life Altering Discovery, not everyone has a soul

What if not everyone has a soul? What if, of those who now have a soul, not everyone will be able to keep their soul once they die? Would you like to know how to keep yours? This book will show you, not only how to keep your soul, but also how to progressively attain conscious immortality.

Not everyone will be able to keep their soul once they die because there are more ways to lose our soul and only one way to retain it. Our soul is the one talent Christ spoke of. It is the seed dropped within us at birth as a word of God.

> Will this seed fall by the wayside where birds will devour it?
> Will it fall on hard rock where it will be scorched by heat?
> Will it fall among thorns where it will choke and suffocate?
> Or will it fall on fertile soil, establish a root system and

grow to become a magnificent tree attracting the birds of the sky?

The most critical knowledge we need to have while living is how to preserve our soul so that once we die, we do not lose it. Our soul does not need to be saved from sin, for the soul never sins. It does not need to be saved from hell, suffering or eternal damnation, for the soul can never suffer. Only the physical body with its mind and emotions can suffer.

What the soul needs to be saved from is annihilation, extinction and loss forever. This will happen, according to the Parable of the Talents, if we do not invest in ourselves and cultivate our minds and hearts. We need to nurture the seed of soul and allow it to establish a root system, grow and blossom.

We are gifted with free choice. We all possess a most valuable treasure, our soul. Will we pursue trivia and squander our chance to cultivate this treasure? Or will we polish this most valuable of gems so its brilliance, brightness and light shines from the mountaintop so everyone can see it and be guided to find their way home.

This book will give us the knowledge and the resources we need to not only preserve
our soul, but to cultivate it until we finally attain conscious immortality.

2. Secret Teachings of Christ, based on the parables

The secret teachings of Christ were reserved for His disciples only. Now, for the first time, they are being revealed to you. This insightful, eye-opening book will forever change how you view Christ and His parables. The Secret Teachings of Christ is a breakthrough in revealing what Christ really wanted us to know. Not only did Christ hide His most crucial teachings in the parables, He also bestowed upon us three life-altering gifts: why we should **accept and love ourselves**, why we should know that **we are important,** and that **we can make a difference**. Knowing these will surely boost our self-esteem.

The parables appear to be simple stories that Christ told His listeners. They are encoded with hidden gems of truth that He could not reveal openly lest He be stoned and killed prematurely. The parables are a clever way to preserve His teachings for posterity. The time has come to reveal these truths openly and for all. This book reveals the secret teachings of Christ based on the parables. Some of the topics include:

> What lessons can we learn from the parable of the lamp? •What does John the Baptist symbolize? •Why can't we mix new and old garments? •Who are Beelzebub and Satan? •Where is the most fertile soil to sow spiritual seeds and who is the Sower? •What exactly is the Kingdom of Heaven? Is it within us? How do we find and use it? Why is the Kingdom of Heaven like a seed, yeast, a treasure, a pearl and a net? How can discovering the Kingdom Within transform our lives? •Why did Christ have 12 disciples? •Why would a shepherd leave 99 of his sheep to seek the one he lost? •Why must we forgive? •How can we double the talents we are entrusted with? •Who is the Prodigal Son who returns home? •Did Christ come to die for our sins? Or did we kill Him because of our sins? •Why would Christ expect a barren fig tree to produce figs? •What "fertilizer" can we use to be productive ourselves? •Why does Christ refer to "wedding feasts" in His parables? Who are invited to these feasts? •What is the significance of the numbers Christ used in His parables? •Why 10 virgins? •Why is the parable of The Good Samaritan so important? •Who is our neighbor? •What does "midnight" refer to in the parables? •Is it possible to be rich and be saved? •Are Heaven and Hell real places? •What secrets lie hidden in The Lord's Last Supper? •What does the life of Jesus Christ tell us about our lives?

For a very long time a veil has been placed over our

eyes so we cannot see clearly. Ignorance, bias, presupposition and entrenched beliefs are components of this veil. We are responsible for our lives. If the truth is important to know, then we must do the work. We must seek, ask and knock until we have a satisfactory answer. This book will give us the knowledge we need to change course for an enlightened life.

3. Know Yourself, Love Yourself and Express Yourself

If you truly know yourself, you will love yourself and if you love yourself, you will express yourself. This perceptive, empowering book will show you how.

Is there a treasure that never spoils buried deep within us? Is this treasure a "talent" that we must develop? What exactly is this "talent"? How can we find it?

Developing this "talent" is our number one priority. It is the one thing that we must seek at the expense of all else. If we gain the whole world but do not discover what this "talent" is, we have wasted our life pursuing trivia. This "talent" is a secret hidden in plain view. Unless we know where to look, we will not see it. It is in Christianity and it is the Philosopher's Stone that the Alchemists were seeking.

Our lives would be simple had we been born with a guide for living, but we are not. We do not know why we are here, what we need to do with our lives or why we contract diseases, suffer and die. Yet, we can have meaningful answers for all of our questions. This book provides answers. It also demonstrates that we are not simply a physical body; we have astral and spiritual bodies as well. All three bodies must be cared for and nurtured so they can grow and blossom.

This book explains the purpose of life, provides a guide for intentional living and reveals many secrets such as the secret of Christianity, the secret of the Alchemists, the secrets of sleep and dreams, the secret of prayer, the secret of the mustard seed, the secret of the breath and the secret of the Millennium. Knowing these secrets will open our eyes and our hearts. We will know who we are and what we need to do with our lives. Our journey begins when we know ourselves intimately, love ourselves unconditionally and express ourselves fearlessly.

Some of the topics include:

>A Manual for Living •Does Life have a Purpose? •Why Are We Born, Live and Die? •We Are in a Theater •We Are on a Journey •We Are a Work in Progress •We Are Connected •The Nature of Our Earthly Experiences •We Are a Trinity •I AM •Knowing Our Source •The Three Names of God •How Can We Know for Certain? •Concepts of Self •Accept Yourself •Forgive Yourself •Love Yourself •Love Others •The Nature of Love •The Quest for Happiness •Be Prepared, Always •Be Fearless •Highlight Your Uniqueness •Sharpen Your Toolset •Express Yourself •Secret of Christianity •Secret of the Mustard Seed •Secret of Prayer •Secret of Sleep and Dreams •Secret of the Breath •Secret of the Alchemists •Secret of the Millennium

4. Mystery Solved! human immortality revealed

What if suddenly we understood the mysteries of life and death? Why were we born? Why do we age and die? Why do we experience pain and suffering? Why does evil exist? What if we knew that our birth was not an accident? That there is a plan for our lives and this plan is of our own choosing? What if we knew why we are attracted to specific individuals, places and situations, but not by others? What if we discovered that we have a soul and that it is of the nature of God? What if we had a better understanding of what this nature is? Would any of this make a difference? How would having answers impact our lives?

This book is based on personal experience and has the power to transform our lives for the better. The revelation I received can be yours. Peace, serenity and understanding await you. Some of the topics include:

The Human Experience •Touching Heaven •The Spark •Reflection •Dream, The Assembly •Clues About the Nature of My Self •The Miraculous •Revelation •Disadvantages of Same Body Physical Immortality •Advantages of Cyclic Immortality •Elegance of Cyclic Immortality •What Constitutes Proof? •The Evidence •Soul, Fact or Fiction •What is Soul? •Evidence in Support of Soul •Why Do Cells Divide •Birth, Where Do We Come From? •Why Don't We Remember? •Death, Where Do We Go After We Die? •Does Life Have a Purpose? •Why Attraction? •Why Do We Experience Misery, Pain and Suffering? •Where Does Our Sense of Wonder Come From? •Why Do We Dream? •The Mystery of Identity •Understanding the Nature of Life •Making the Most of This Life •Planning for Our Next Life

The Human Experience is *unique.* Make the most of it by unravelling its mysteries. The greatest gift we have is freedom of choice. We can choose to live governed by random forces where we deal with whatever happens, or we can consciously take control of our lives. We are given "talents" and placed on a stage. We are expected to invest our talents wisely. This book will help us do just that. Act and take charge. A small investment on your part will yield a great return.

5. Listening to the Voice Within, becoming enlightened

Learning to listen to the Voice Within is the shortest route to living the abundant life. This book will show us how this practice will place us on an accelerated path to finding and living our mission in life.

There is one "gift" without which we cease to be human. Plants and animals do not have it. Only humans have it. Most do not appreciate this trademark of being human or use it effectively to advance their "Happiness Quotient." In fact, many use it to their detriment. We can discover, cultivate and learn to use this gift more effectively. It requires us to be fearless, open-minded and intent on improving our lot in life. This gift is our conscience coupled with Freedom of Choice.

Listening to The Voice Within will show us how to best use our Free Will. This book will inform, empower and liberate us. It is a guide for transformation. It will help us become enlightened beings. It will push us to grow beyond our comfort zone. To grow, we must break loose of the tethers that constrict and stifle us. Life is a journey, not a destination. If we open our minds and hearts to reason and inspiration and listen to the promptings of The Voice Within, we can be transformed. We need to discover who we are spiritually, in addition to what we are materially. Our journey of awakening starts when we let go of our fears and learn to exercise our freedom of choice. We are responsible for our lives and the decisions we make. This book is full of empowering and liberating insights that have the potential to change our lives. Here are some of the topics presented in this book:

> What is the Voice Within? •Life as an Experiment •How Free Am I? •My Life as a Garden •Obey or Disobey •Am I My Brother's Keeper? •Privilege •The Transient and the Enduring •Journey to Enough •The Path Less Travelled •Energy, Force, & Power •Human Pyramid •Natural "Enemies" of Humanity •Memory as a Photograph •Good, Bad and Evil •Transformers of the World •Perfection •Why Attraction? Why Love? •Insights I Live by •Self-Examination •Questions to Consider •Aging, Life and Death •Mystery of Dreams •Raising Our Consciousness •Soul •Who Am I? •The Word Made Flesh •As Within, So Without •In God's Image •Living in Truth •When Two

or More Come Together •Good News and Sad News •Thy Kingdom Come! •The Second Coming •Brave, Enlightened World

Our journey of awakening starts when we let go of our fears and act with intelligence. The first decision we have to make is whether or not we are serious about improving the quality of our life by gaining knowledge and understanding. Once we are equipped with the right knowledge, we can act boldly. It will make a difference in how you see and interpret the events in your life.

6. The Hidden Meaning & Power of the Lord's Prayer, based on the Syriac Aramaic

The Lord's Prayer is the only specific prayer Christ asked to learn and recite. Why? This book will reveal the hidden gems within the Lord's Prayer. It will also share a 12-step process to effective prayer and how to make sure our prayers are heard and answered. Additionally, this book will explain a spiritual perspective on how to establish the kingdom of heaven in our lives. Some of the topics include:

> ***Our Father who art in heaven.*** Who is this Father we are praying to? And where exactly is this heaven? •***Hallowed be Thy Name.*** Do we know God's name so that we may hallow it? How can we find out what this name is? •***Thy kingdom come.*** What exactly is this kingdom and why are we asking for it to come? Is the Kingdom of God the same as the Kingdom of Heaven? •***Thy will be done on earth as it is in heaven.*** What does this mean? What is God's will in heaven that we want it done on earth as well? Is there any other will than that of God's will? •***Give us this day our daily bread.*** Why are we asking only for bread? What about some meat and potatoes as well? How about some dessert while we are at it? Does this mean we do not have to earn our livelihood? •***And lead us not into temptation.***

Who leads us into temptation? Is it God or the Devil? If it is the Devil, why are we asking God not to lead us into temptation? ●*But deliver us from evil.* What exactly is evil? And if God does deliver us from evil, does it mean that we do not face difficulties anymore? ●Why did Christ teach us this specific prayer? What hidden gems buried within it that we need to discover?

7. A Passion for Living, a path to meaning and joy

Not much can be achieved in life without passion. Following our passion, we live a meaningful and joyous life. What can be more rewarding!

Do you know why we are here and what is the best way to live? Are we the result of an accident of nature? Were we created by God to be tested? We can have real and satisfying answers to these fundamental questions. The key is insistent desire, persistence and a demand to know. **"Ask and it will be given to you; seek and you will find; knock and the door will be opened for you."** Matt 7:7-8. This is what Christ promised us. These are active verbs. We must take the first steps. Our asking, seeking and knocking, however, must be loud, insistent and persistent until we have our answer.

To live a life of meaning and joy, we must wake up to who we are. We must live for a purpose that embodies who we want to be. We can be victimized by our circumstances or we can choose to create the life we want. This book helps us wake up, decide on something worthwhile to live for, know ourselves, decipher the meaning of life and master the art of living. We can understand why we age and die, how to release our brakes, take it easy, do what we can and enjoy ourselves. If we apply the insights in this book, we will discover our passion for living and live a life of meaning and joy.

Some of the topics in this book include:

> Wakeful Living ●We Do Not Have to Struggle to Succeed

•We Have What It Takes •Have Something Worthwhile to Live For •Know Yourself •Decipher the Meaning of Life and Master the Art of Living •The Blueprint of Life and Its Architect •Understand Why We Age and Die •Eight Reasons We Decide to Die •Release Your Brakes •Ignorance, Fear, Pain and Suffering •Take it Easy, Enjoy Yourself and Do What You Can •Living Like a Corporation •Willingness to Change •Dimensions of Reality

To face the challenges of life, we need knowledge stemming from experience. If knowledge is power, these books give us the power we need to live happy, fulfilled and meaningful lives. Instead of merely passing through life, we can wake up, live with passion and make a positive difference in our lives and the lives of others. By improving the quality of our life through knowledge, the lives of those we touch will also improve. We are each valuable because we are interconnected. If J. T. through one book altered the course of my life for the better, we can do the same.

Grab this opportunity to set your life on a new course. This is your chance. Order these books and study them. You will gain understanding and valuable insight on how to master your circumstances. With understanding comes wisdom, contentment and peace of mind. You have the power, not only to improve your life, but also to impact the lives of those you care about. Often, all it takes is a small gesture such as the gift of a valuable book.

ACKNOWLEDGEMENT

I am grateful to the Cosmic for inspiration, guidance and the required time to write this book. I appreciate the help of all those who made this book a reality especially my wife Barbara. I am indebted for her reviewing and editing. Barbara's help and support have been invaluable. Next, I would like to thank family and friends for their continued support, especially Joe Shammas for his review and suggestions.

ABOUT THE AUTHOR

Shahan Shammas

Shahan was born in Aleppo, Syria. At the age of 15, he went to Lebanon where he entered a monastery to study and prepare to be a monk. After two years in the monastery, he left to continue his education. Shahan graduated from the American University of Beirut with a Bachelor's degree in Biology. At the age of 24, Shahan left for the United States and became a US citizen after serving three years in the Army at the medical laboratory of Fort Meade, Md. After working as an Electron Microscopist at the Walter Reed Army Medical Center for 7 years, Shahan started a new career in Information Systems. He worked for the Treasury Department until he retired. Shahan then became a teacher at the Judy Hoyer Family Learning Center where he taught Life Skills to adults for ten years. Shahan's background is in the Sciences, Religion, Philosophy and Spirituality. Shahan has lectured extensively in the areas of acquiring knowledge, raising consciousness and actualizing the human potential.

Shahan Shammas is a cultivator of the mind. He has dedicated his life to learning and teaching. His purpose is to be a light that dispels darkness, to empower those he encounters, and to be an agent for peace.

www.ingramcontent.com/pod-product-compliance
Lightning Source LLC
Chambersburg PA
CBHW060459090426
42735CB00011B/2040